CONCILIUM

Religion in the Eighties

CONCILIUM

Concilium 149 (9/1981): Spirituality

FRANCIS OF ASSISI TODAY

Edited by

Christian Duquoc

and

Casiano Floristán

English Language Editor
Marcus Lefébure

T. & T. CLARK LTD.
Edinburgh

THE SEABURY PRESS
New York

November 1981

T. & T. Clark Ltd., 36 George Street, Edinburgh EH2 2LQ
ISBN: 0 567 30029 3

The Seabury Press, 815 Second Avenue, New York, N.Y. 10017
ISBN: 0 8164 2349 0

Library of Congress Catalog Card No.: 80 54391

Printed in Scotland by William Blackwood & Sons Ltd., Edinburgh

Concilium: Monthly except July and August
Subscriptions 1981: All countries (except U.S.A. and Canada) £27·00 postage and handling included; U.S.A. and Canada $64.00 postage and handling included. (Second class postage licence 541-530 at New York, N.Y.) Subscription distribution in U.S. by Expediters of the Printed Word Ltd., 527 Madison Avenue, Suite 1217, New York, N.Y. 10022.

CONTENTS

v

Conclusion

Editorial

FRANCIS OF ASSISI is not just anybody, he is a legendary hero and a popular saint. The celebration of the eight-hundredth anniversary of his birth invites us to pit our own time against the epic of the medieval saint. Our aim in this issue is not to be scientifically critical, although we intend to be that too; it is to tell Christians about a legend that is rooted in an action the relevance of which is not just a matter of a scholar's fancy. It is intended to invite conversion rather than to provide information. We do not contemplate Francis for the beauty of his life, we follow in his footsteps. All the articles in this issue agree on this practical end.

I have talked about the *legend* of Francis, not about the illusion or the dream. Francis' life is rooted in a world in travail: the feudal system is spent, the commercial cities have the future before them. Francis lives at the hinge of two worlds. *J. le Goff* outlines for us the social context in which the legend is born, the legend that is the social and literary precipitate of his activity. The breakdown of the feudal world, the explosion of the ravenous hunger of commerce should not hide from us another aspect of the medieval West: the constant awareness of the Muslim peril. Christendom feels that it is besieged by armies that occupy the land of Jesus' birth and block access to his tomb. By liberating his sepulchre, Christians restore to Christ his royalty over a world challenged by Islam. The combat between the two religions comes to take on the proportions of the cosmic conflict between Good and Evil. Each side is convinced it is defending God's cause. *F. de Beer* deploys vast erudition and evangelical enthusiasm to bring out Francis' originality in this apocalyptic drama: the meeting of Francis and the Sultan marks the dawning of a new understanding of Christianity. It was, however, too novel for their contemporaries to be able to take it in.

Part of situating Francis in his milieu is disengaging the axes that determine the originality of his attitude and which gave rise to the legend. We have deemed three axes in particular worth mentioning: the poverty that *M. Mollat* deals with, the evangelisation and the communities that *N. Fabbretti* studies, and the recovery of the original tang of Scripture which *T. Desbonnets* brings out.

It is on the basis of this originality of Francis in these three domains that we can begin to measure the contemporary relevance of what he did so long ago. *B. Duclos* attributes the continuing fascination of Francis to his attachment to the gospel: he followed Christ so intimately that believers could almost identify them. The stigmata are the witness of this conviction. *A. Rotzetter* and *K. Walf* establish the limits of this relevance, without, however, denying its positive force.

It is critical theology that is in the ascendent nowadays, and it is not prepared to take hold of the Christian significance of actions attributed to figures now lost for ever. It is perhaps necessary to find a way taking better hold of the power of conversion and even of subversion contained in the remembrance of the actions of the saints, as crystallised in legend. In any case Francis has left us two traces of himself: his legend and the orders which claim to be his heirs. What would the heirs be without the legend? But would there be a legend if nobody claimed the heritage?

CHRISTIAN DUQUOC
CASIANO FLORISTÁN

PART I

His Context

Jacques le Goff

Francis of Assisi between the Renewals and Restraints of Feudal Society

FRANCIS OF ASSISI was born in the middle of a period of great upsurge in the medieval West, and in a region where this upsurge was at its strongest.

For modern historians, the first signs of this upsurge were demographic and economic in character. From about the year 1000, there was a sharp increase in population—unequally spread, but continuing regularly, with some real 'population explosions', as in northern and central Italy—leading to a doubling of the population over the next two hundred years. All these people had to be fed, materially and spiritually.

Progress was at first rural progress in a society where everything was based on the land. It was general and quantitative: a great movement of land clearance opened up new areas of cultivation; open spaces appeared or were enlarged in the forest covering Christian Europe. Solitude had to be sought farther afield. There was qualitative progress also, but this hardly touched the rocky escarpments of Francis' birthplace: the wheeled cart and the asymmetrical ploughshare replaced the earlier shallower plough in the plains; the invention of the horse collar allowed the more powerful horse to replace the ox in agriculture, new crops were introduced on the three-field rotation system, fields were levelled and irrigated, increasing the number of animals that could be pastured on them; but all this only just affected mountainous Umbria. There too, however, the number of mills increased, introducing the beginnings of mechanisation into the hills and valleys of the region. The increased population began to group together in villages, clusters of dwellings around and often clinging to the local church and manor: the process of *incastellamento*.

The most notable consequence of the population and economic upswing was a powerful trend to urbanisation. More decisive than the superficial urbanisation of the Greco-Roman world, more like the later waves of urban explosion in the nineteenth and twentieth centuries, this created a network of towns which, unlike those of classical times or even the high middle ages, were economic, political and cultural centres rather than military or economic ones. To take just one of the results of this urban phenomenon in the religious field: in the course of the thirteenth century, the figure of the holy bishop holding episcopal power in the old-style towns disappeared from Italy,

3

though still to be found in less urbanised England. From now on, holiness was to belong to those who either accepted the fact of the towns: holy bourgeois, holy lay people, holy mendicant friars; or rejected it: holy hermits.

Towns became work sites where division of labour led to a multiplicity of trades, giving rise, in the three sectors advancing towards 'industrialisation'—building, textiles and tanning—to a 'pre-proletarian' workforce, defenceless against the subordination of the 'just wage' to the 'fair price', which simply meant the price determined by the laws of supply and demand, and against domination by employers. They became exchanges where fairs and markets flourished under the impetus of business whose influence spread locally and farther afield, giving more and more weight to the merchants who controlled the various forms of exchange. Towns were the chief focuses of economic exchange which brought an ever-growing need for a basic means of exchange: money. The dealers of this fragmented Christendom with numerous money systems in operation soon created a new breed of specialists in money: the money changers, who were to develop into bankers, taking this function away from the monasteries, who had been able to provide the low level of credit needed by the smaller transactions of the high middle ages, and from the Jews, who were henceforth confined to cash lenders, i.e., 'usurers', as were a growing number of Christian merchants. The centres of the money market, the towns also became the centres of the labour market, where the numbers of employees steadily increased.

As economic centres, the towns also became the new power centres. Beside and, sometimes, over against the traditional power of the bishop and the lord of the manor, sometimes the same person, a new class, the citizens or bourgeoisie won themselves 'freedoms', privileges on an ever-increasing scale. Without overturning the economic and political pillars of the feudal system, they brought a variant into it, introducing freedom (*stadtluft macht frei*, as the Germans say), and equality before the law (the civic or communal vow uniting equals in law). They created a society in which economic and social inequality was no longer based on birth, on family, but on fortune counted in land and possessions, owning ground and buildings in the towns, earning rates and taxes in the shape of money.

As in more recent phases of widespread urbanisation, medieval towns were full of new or established immigrants, with a high turnover in their numbers. Their inhabitants were rootless, immigrant peasants.

By the time Francis of Assisi was born, this new society was just getting past its period of uncontrolled growth, of wild exuberance, and moving into the institutional-ised phase, which happened in Italy rather sooner than elsewhere, both as regards the corporations of craftsmen and merchants (*arti*) and political organisations (*communes*). To take a symbolic example from Perugia, Assisi's great rival at the time, the first known building of the Commune, the Palace of the Consuls (later known as the Palace of the *Potestat*), dates from 1205, when Francis was twenty-three.

Peasant society was also on the move at the same time. Even though a large part of the rural population was being sucked into the towns in the process of *inurbamento*, those who stayed in the country obtained franchises, and, in the case of serfs, liberty, from their feudal lords. But these lords' reaction to the growing economic hold of the towns over their rural domains and their own resulting financial problems, led to a system of economic exploitation bearing on most strata of rural society.

The Church and ecclesiastical society, in and faced with this new situation, were in some ways the first to change. What is known as the Gregorian reform, which in fact both in time and content spread beyond the pontificate of Gregory VII (1073-85), was more than a process of freeing the ranks of the clergy from feudal lay domination. Of course, the emancipation of the Holy See from the imperial power, the increasing freedom from powerful lay influence in the election of bishops and abbots, were significant developments, as were the efforts to eliminate all the economic and social pressures that could be grouped under the general heading of Simony. The struggle against everything represented by 'Nicolaitarism' was basic; the struggle against the sexual incontinence of the clergy was not merely a moral and spiritual advance: by forbidding the first of the three orders defined by the tripartite scheme of *oratores, bellatores* and *laboratores* at the beginning of the eleventh century to marry or live in concubinage, the Church was placing a definite sexual frontier between clergy and laity.

The Gregorian reform was also a desire to return to source—*Ecclesiae primitiva forma*—and to follow the apostolic example—*Vita vere apostolica*. A realisation of the vices into which Christian society—clerical as well as lay—had fallen, brought a new impetus to the process of Christianisation. There was also a feeling that the year 1000 had brought 'a new Spring to the world' (G. Duby). This inspiration was communicated to the world at large through peace-making initiatives. The Gregorian reform was in a sense the institutionalisation of this inspiration and the means by which it permeated all levels of society in the course of the twelfth century.

But reform of the Church was also a response to the way the world was evolving, an effort to adapt to outside events. This response was made on the institutional level in the first place, and had three main thrusts: the establishment of new religious orders, the growth of the canonical movement, and the acceptance of plurality within the Church.

The new orders made themselves out to be a return to the original Benedictine rule through emphasis on manual labour—which re-established its place alongside the *opus dei*—and stress on simplicity of life, seen as much in the rejection of traditional forms of monastic wealth as in the plain architectural and artistic styles evolved as a contrast to the exuberant sculpture, miniatures and precious metal work of the Romanesque. Of the two most important new orders, one, the Carthusians, founded by Bruno in 1084, aimed for a primitive eremitical style, and then, under Guigues II, prior from 1173-80, for an ascesis composed of four 'spiritual degrees': reading, meditation, prayer and contemplation; the other, the Cistercians, founded by Robert de Molesme in 1098 and inspired by St Bernard, abbot of Clairvaux from 1115-53, combined economic success with spiritual reform. The Cistercian 'desert' was to be found in valleys where the Order set up its mills and—making use of mechanisation to allow more time to concentrate on spiritual matters—played its part in technological advance, particularly in the field of metallurgy, while adapting itself to the new rural economy, especially in the development of pasturing and wool production, and by setting up a new type of exploitation: tithe barns.

If reformed monasticism found a better balance between manual work and prayer, the canonical movement brought about a new balance between the active and the contemplative life, between the *cura animarum* and community life. Though the canons established at Prémontré by Norbert de Xanten in 1120 continued in a rural setting, where they practised poverty, manual labour (they were great land clearers) and preaching, most of the canons in the twelfth century were tied to an urban environment. The adoption of the very open and flexible rule known as Augustinian, which had originally been conceived in an urban environment—though that of Augustine's day was very different from that of the twelfth century—allowed the Augustinian canons to combine community life, individual asceticism and parish work.

The *Liber de diversis ordinibus et professionibus quae sunt in Ecclesia*, written between 1125 and 1130, probably by a canon of Liège, which was either left unfinished or has come down to us in an incomplete manuscript, gives an account of the multiplicity of statutes affecting clerics and religious, and allows for the plurality of ecclesial institutions, on the pattern of the Father's 'house' in which there are 'many mansions'. It classifies these statutes according to their degree of removal from the world and distance from places of human residence: 'some are completely set apart from the masses . . .

some are set up alongside people; others live in the midst of other people'.

Lay society was taking an increasingly active part in religious life, and despite the maintenance of the divide between clergy and laity, the latter strengthened their presence in the religious field. In the new orders, lay brothers or converts played a growing role. The military orders brought about a sort of fusion between religious and warrior, the religious life and the code of chivalry. Pietist groups, starting in Picardy and Flanders—Bégards and Béguines—then spreading to the foothills of the Alps, were set up with the encouragement of clerics like the Liège priest Lambert le Bègue, who died in 1177, and the famous preacher Jacques de Vitry, who was to write a life of the Béguine recluse Marie d'Oignies before becoming bishop of Acre and later cardinal. Towards 1200, groups of *laici religiosi* and *mulieres religiosae* were increasing fast. The Pataria of Milan and its successors in the twelfth century brought clergy and laity seeking reform together. A council held in Milan in the winter of 1177 on the initiative of the archbishop and the consuls assembled, in a field at the gates of the town, 'an enormous crowd of clergy and lay people anxious to bury the vices and encourage the virtues'. During the 1140s, the regular canon, Arnold of Brescia, who had formerly inveighed against the corrupt life of the clergy of his native town, roused the lay people of Rome in a reform movement that was both religious and political.

Faced with this changing world, the Church sought new doctrinal formulations, new religious practices. The most important area of doctrinal evolution was that concerning sin and the sacraments. Theologians, often of opposing schools, such as the masters of the episcopal school of Laon, Anselm and William of Champeaux, and the Parisian Abelard, worked out a voluntarist doctrine of sin which looked for its causes in the individual conscience. From now on, intention was to be the essential ingredient. This quest for intention brought about a new practice in the sacrament of penance. The old public form of penance had fallen into disuse, and it would appear that a gap had opened up between this old public form and the new forms of private confession, filled with a variety of individual or collective penitential practices. In the twelfth century, there was apparently a growing tendency to individual auricular confession alongside traditional penitential practice. This development was made obligatory by the Canon *Omnis utriusque sexus* of the Fourth Lateran Council of 1215, which required all the faithful of both sexes to make a private confession at least once a year. The admission of guilt became more important than the penance imposed, and a pioneering element was introduced into people's consciousness: examination of conscience.

This renewed form of penance took its place in a new concept of the sacraments, a seven-fold structure which fitted into a new system which also included seven capital sins and the seven gifts of the Holy Ghost. One interesting line of study would be the changing hierarchy of values accorded to individual items in these lists of seven. For instance, *avaritia*, the vice that goes with a monetary economy, came to occupy first place among the seven deadly sins instead of *superbia*, the vice particularly associated with *feudalism*.

A similar evolution was at work in the field of concepts and practices of justice. The predominant concern was to find degrees of punishment appropriate to faults and crimes seen not only in themselves but also in relation to the situation and intentions of those who committed them.

The last change, of supreme importance, was in the field of learning. The growth of the towns first brought about an expansion of certain episcopal schools, such as those of Laon, Chartres and Paris. But this renewal was only a straw in the wind, and the monastic schools were also giving their last flickers of light. New town schools were springing up in a somewhat haphazard fashion, concentrating on two main subjects. One was theology, which appealed above all to the intellectual, social and political circles flourishing in Paris. The other was law, pre-eminently as a result of the commune structure growing up in Bologna. Two works which were to become classics were produced within a few years of each other, the *Decretum* of Gratian towards 1140, and the four volumes of the *Sententiae* by the bishop of Paris, the Italian, Peter Lombard, between 1155 and 1160. Both these illustrate a new intellectual environment, that of specialists in theological or juridical theory, and a new method, based on discussion and logical reasoning, that of scholasticism.

This great change in the Church brought a return of 'ecumenical' councils to the West, after centuries without any general councils. The four Lateran Councils, of 1123, 1139, 1179 and 1215 were at once the completion of the Gregorian reform and the Church's attempt at *aggiornamento* in the face of a century of great changes. But their results were ambiguous, as was the triumph of papal power whose expression they were. As well as adapting to new ideas, they sought to stem—if not to block completely—their advance. And despite its efforts at *aggiornamento*, the Church of the beginning of the thirteenth century was still subject to a number of restraints, both inherited and newly imposed.

In particular, it failed to appreciate the economic revolution and the urban society it produced, and stayed stuck in rural feudalism. It also made rapid strides in the direction of stultifying new structures: the new Orders, particularly the Cistercians, were distracted into acquiring wealth, exploited lay brothers, became bogged down in their country settings; the all-pervading canon law imposed a dessicating juridicism; the degeneration into bureaucracy and autocracy of the papacy and the Roman curia also began to make themselves felt.

The Church experienced some revealing setbacks, such as the Crusades, which proved incapable of stemming the Muslim tide, or of following their original aims, as was shown by the detour of the fourth Crusade to Constantinople. It was incapable of kindling the earlier enthusiasms, particularly for the struggle against heretics inside Christendom itself. Finally, it proved ill adapted, or even powerless, to contain or canalise the challenges of history: the monetary aggression, new forms of violence, the contradictory aspirations of Christians to enjoy more of the goods of the world on one hand, while inveighing more against desires for riches, power and the pleasures of the flesh on the other.

While scholasticism and the new canon law provided the Church with the means of applying theory to the new situations emerging in Christian society, and the works popularising their findings—manuals for confessors, collections of model sermons and of *exempla*—provided unlearned priests with the means of meeting the new requirements of the faithful, at least in part, these learned constructs also contributed to a widening of the cultural gap between an ecclesiastical elite and an unlettered mass of the laity. They also served to stifle, distort or take over the renaissance of popular culture which occurred in the thirteenth century.

Feudalism had become monarchical, and the ruling culture had been influenced by the dominant lay classes, the aristocracy and the knights, whose system of courtly values had been imposed on the emergent society, even the urban society of the Italian communes. Francis of Assisi himself felt the influence of this chivalresque culture, and his cult of poverty had courtly overtones. His chivalresque dream, embodied in his vision of the house full of weapons, never completely vanished from his mind. Lady Poverty did indeed represent a rejection of the economic and social values of aristocratic and bourgeois society, but this rejection was based on a courtly, feudal model. In his *De nugis curialum* of 1192-3, the Englishman, Walter Map deplored the way the clergy were being sucked into the whirlpool of vice and futility of the princely courts. At the same time, the bishop of Paris, Maurice de Sully, despite his own—exceptional—humble origins, could preach a sermon—in Latin and the vernacular—recalling peasants to their duties of paying tithes to the Church and rents to their landlords.

Gabriel le Bras has made a shrewd comment on the ecclesiastical proliferation of the twelfth century: 'By a curious chance, the multiplication of clerical modes in no way corresponded to the needs of the century: rather did it correspond to the needs of the rich for salvation (or for pomp) and to the (sometimes excessive) comforts of the canons and priests'.

No setback suffered by the Church at the end of the twelfth century is more significant than its failure to cope with the movement of frankly heretical (or classed by the Church as such) lay people. The most spectacular and serious of these movements was undoubtedly Catharism which affected the lower Rhine basin and parts of France and the Empire from the Loire to the Alps, particularly southern France, Provence and northern Italy. This was a failure of the local clergy and of the Cistercians, to whom the pope had entrusted the regulation of preaching after the Crusades. Its consequences were a war waged by the Church within Christendom, the lasting division between the South of France and the North, and the setting-up of the Inquisition—one of the greatest crimes committed against humanity in history.

Worse still, perhaps, was the incomprehension, the fear, even, shown by the Church in the face of movements of *laici religiosi* who did not profess any heretical doctrine. Canon 26 of the second Lateran Council had already forbidden any form of monastic religious life practised by devout women in their own homes. The cases of the Waldenses and the *Humiliati* were still more serious. The first were poor people of Lyons who had responded to the summons of one, Peter Waldo, a wealthy merchant there, and who, towards 1170, began to devote their lives to prayer and good works, reading the Bible, preaching and begging. In Milan towards 1175, a group of tradespeople formed themselves into a community, the *Humiliati*, also devoting their lives to work and prayer, reading the Bible in the vernacular and preaching. They were soon swarming all over Lombardy. At Verona in 1184, Pope Lucius III excommunicated Cathars, Waldenses and *Humiliati* at one fell swoop. What were they being condemned for? Basically, for taking over a clerical monopoly, that of preaching. Walter Map, as an ecclesiastical dignitary (he was an archdeacon at Oxford), was one of the first to protest against this new scandal: 'Like a pearl cast before swine, shall the Word be given to ignorant people whom we know to be incapable of receiving it, let alone of giving back what they have received?'. This usurpation was made all the more scandalous in his eyes by the fact that it was being carried out not only by lay men, but also by lay *women*.

It is true that Innocent III made some amends and from 1190 won back some of the *Humiliati* by changing them into 'orders', grouping them into three orders of which the first two were made up of genuine religious living according to a rule, with the third comprising a sort of 'third order before its time', made up of those who practised a trade to supply their wants and to earn money that could be given to the poor. In the same way, Innocent III also made a distinction in Scripture between *aperta*, narrative and moralising passages accessible to all, and *profonda*, dogmatic statements whose understanding and explanation were reserved to the clergy.

So towards the year 1200, certain lay circles had these stirrings, needs and demands: direct access to the Scriptures, without the barrier of Latin or the intervention of the clergy; the right to the ministry of the Word; the right to practise the religious life in accordance with the needs of the times, within their own families, callings and lay state. To which one must add the aspiration to equality between the sexes professed at the end of the twelfth century by the *Humiliati* of Lombardy, the rural penitents of northern Italy, and the Bégards and Béguines in the northern parts of France and the Empire.

Some people, such as the Calabrian priest, Joaquim de Fiore, saw no hope till a third age dawned in the world, an age of the Holy Spirit following those of the Father and the Son, and ushering in a community of 'people of the spirit', which they themselves might have to bring into being through recourse to 'active or even revolutionary steps'.

This was the context in which Francis of Assisi reached the age of twenty, in 1201 or 1202. His success was to reside in the way he responded to the aspirations of a large number of his contemporaries, both in what they accepted and in what they rejected. He was a child of the town, a merchant's son, and the town was to be his first mission field. But he tried to give the town a feeling for poverty instead of for money and other forms of wealth, a sense of peace to replace the continual internecine strife he knew in Assisi, between Assisi and Perugia.

Rediscovering the spirit of St Martin in a new context, he looked for alternation between the bustle of the town and the hermit's retreat, between the wide scope of an apostolate to the world and regeneration in and through solitude. To this settling, establishment society, he showed the open road, he proposed pilgrimage.

A layman at a time that had witnessed the canonisation of a lay merchant, Hombon of Cremona, by the new Pope Innocent in 1199, he tried to show that lay people too can lead a truly apostolic life, like the clergy and with the clergy. Despite the setbacks and humiliations it inflicted on him, he remained faithful to the Church, out of humility and veneration for the sacraments whose administration required a body of differentiated, respected ministers. But significantly, in his brotherhood and as far as possible in his growing Order, he rejected hierarchy and clericalism. In a world where the nuclear family based on the marriage bond was beginning to appear, but in which anti-feminism was still rife and children were neglected, his ties with several women, starting with St Clare, who remained close to him, and his exaltation of the infant Jesus in the crib at Greccio, showed his brotherly concern for women and children.

Without concern for hierarchies, categories or divisions, he put forward one model for all: 'Naked, follow the naked Christ'. In a world of exclusions, through the legislation of the councils, the decrees of canon law, and, in practice, the exclusion of Jews, lepers, heretics, homosexuals; a world in which scholasticism exalted nature in the abstract to the detriment—with some exceptions—of the real world; in this world, he proclaimed—without the least hint of pantheism—the presence of the divine in all creatures. Between the monastic world bathed in its tears and the uncaring masses sunk in an illusory gaiety, he set the joyful face of one who knows that God is joy. He was the contemporary of those smiling gothic angels.

He was also a man of time in his doubts and ambiguities, besides being so in what he accepted and rejected. One major doubt was how the humble life can best live its ideal, through work or through begging. Others were the relationship between voluntary poverty and enforced poverty, and which of them is 'true' poverty; how the apostle, the penitent, should live in society, and what value should be placed on work.

A basic ambiguity is to be found in his views on learning and its relationship to poverty. Is learning not a form of riches, a source of domination and inequality; are books not one of the goods of this world on which the apostle must turn his back? Faced with the intellectual explosion of the day, the university movement in which the Franciscans were soon to be caught up, Francis hesitated. In more general terms, one might ask whether, by the time of his death, Francis had founded the last monastic order or the first modern brotherhood.

Translated by Paul Burns

Short Bibliography

Chapelot J. & Fossier R. *Le Village et la maison au Moyen Age* (Paris 1980).
Chenu M. D. *La Théologie au XIIè siècle* (Paris 1957).

B

Duby G. *L'Économie rurale et la vie des campagnes dans l'Occident médiéval*, 2 vols. (Paris 1962).

Duby G. *Les Trois ordres ou l'imaginaire du féodalisme* (Paris 1978).

Jones Ph. *Economia e società nell' Italia medievale* (Turin 1980).

Le Bras G. 'Le Clergé dans les derniers siècles du Moyen Age', in *Prêtres d'hier et d'aujourd'hui*, Unam Sanctum 28 (Paris 1954).

Little L. K. *Religious Poverty and the Profit Economy in Medieval Europe* (London 1978).

Southern R. S. *Western Society and the Church in the Middle Ages* (Harmondsworth 1970).

Töpfer B. *Das Kommende Reich des Friedens. Zur Entwicklung chiliastischer Zukunftshoffnungen im Hochmittelalter* (Berlin 1964).

Toubert P. *Les Structures du Latium médiéval* (Rome 1973).

Vauchez A. *La Spiritualité du Moyen Age Occidental* (Paris 1975).

Idem. La Sainteté en Occident aux derniers siècles du Moyen Age (Rome 1981).

"La coscienza cittadina nei communi italiani del Duccento" (*Convegni del Centro di Studi sulla spiritualità medievale, XI*) (Todi 1972).

Herésie et Sociétés dans l'Europe pré-industrielle (XIè-XVIIIè siècles) ed. J. le Goff (Paris, The Hague 1972).

I laici nelle "societa christiana" dei secoli XIe XIIe (Mendola 1965).

Storia d'Italia vol 2/1. Dalla caduta dell'Impero Romano al secolo XVIII (Turin 1974).

Francis de Beer

St Francis and Islam

THE STORY of the meeting of St Francis with Sultan Malik al Kamil during the seige of Damietta at the height of the Crusade, long regarded as of doubtful historicity, is today less and less questioned. Nevertheless, even as an indubitable fact, its meaning remains enigmatic for our contemporaries. For many it is a slightly mad provocation, a sudden move, a superb demonstration of disdain for Islam; others regard it as a carefully considered plan and thus a spectacular failure, and still others see it as a new starting point for missionary activity in the Church.

Since the story was ambiguous from the start, it gave rise to a legend according to which Francis had an original idea about the style of the new relationship which had to be established between the two religions whose mutual intolerance made any dialogue impossible or led to an inevitable and unpardonable holy war.

In order to make an orderly progress towards understanding this attitude and verifying its authenticity, we propose to consider it in three states:

1. The complexity of the accounts.
2. An approach to the facts.
3. Francis' assessment.

1. THE COMPLEXITY OF THE ACCOUNTS

The reports about Francis and Islam in the chroniclers and hagiographers of the middle ages can be conveniently divided into those written by outsiders to the order and those written by brethren of the order. The former considers Francis' demand primarily in a political context, even if the politics are ecclesiastical. The latter places it within Francis' personal destiny. More precisely, the first group set the meeting in the context of the Crusade while the second see it as at the heart of the passion of a man in search of martyrdom. Here only a few of the more important sources can be mentioned, but even they offer a rich variety.

(a) The Outsiders

The very first evidence comes from *Jacques de Vitry*, bishop of St John of Acre. De Vitry himself saw Francis in the camp at Damietta in 1219 on his way to the Sultan and

11

this gives his evidence particular value. In his accounts and his letters our chronicler has no scruples about displaying marked hostility towards the Saracens, 'sacrilegious disciples of Antichrist', but the arrival at Damietta 'of the celebrated Brother Francis, beloved of God and men', opens a parenthesis of freshness and strangeness. Driven by an irresistible force, Francis has no sooner arrived at the crusaders' camp than he wants to press on, in spite of all the dangers, to meet the Sultan in person. Against all expectations the Sultan is won over; he listens to the message of Christ with extreme attention. Even his entourage is shaken. After several days of conversation the Sultan finds himself forced, apparently with regret, to send Francis away under strong guard because of his hold on the Sultan's army, but asks him to pray to God for him that God may deign to reveal to him the law and the faith which are most pleasing to him. In short, it was a small success. True, the author makes a point of adding that while the Friars Minor are very well received as long as they preach the gospel, as soon as they set themselves in opposition to Mohammed by calling him a traitor and a liar they are immediately persecuted, but for us this simply emphasises still more the unusual character of the meeting between Francis and the Sultan.

In Francis' own lifetime, or very shortly after his death (1226), another chronicler of the Crusade, *Ernoult*, describes the same interview, but this time in a firmly clerical context. On the side of the crusaders, at the height of the siege of Damietta, Francis has to overcome the suspicion of the papal legate, who allows 'the two clerics' to leave 'at the risk of his life, disclaiming any responsibility'. Francis' action is entirely his own affair. In the Saracen camp, Francis' arrival is first seen by the Sultan as ambiguous: is he coming as a plenipotentiary or as a renegade? Neither, replies Francis. I come simply on behalf of God as someone responsible for your soul. 'If you do not listen to me you are the loser. But if you deign to hear me, I shall prove, by "straight arguments", to you and your counsellors that your law is worthless. If we are unable to prove this, cut off our heads!' The Sultan refuses to discuss before summoning the 'archbishops and clergy of his law'. This little council has hardly met when all the clergy, in the name of that law, not only refuse any discussion but also urge the Sultan to have the heads of the two Christian clerics cut off. The Sultan, touched by the risk run for the salvation of his soul, refuses to accede to his clergy's demand and offers to let Francis remain in Moslem territory in complete security and prosperity. Francis refuses: if no-one will listen to him or discuss with him, he prefers to leave. The only thing he is interested in is the salvation of souls. He takes his leave of the Sultan, who gives him a safe conduct back to the crusaders' camp.

Here too, in this strange confrontation, only the Sultan and Francis meet, despite the hostility of the 'two clergies', both the Christian and the Moslem.

Even more symptomatic is the legend of St Francis in verse (1232) by the poet *Henri d'Avranches*, based on the *Vita I* of Thomas of Celano. Various fantastic prejudices of the time about Islam are in evidence, such as the idea that it is a variant of the characteristic heresy of the Greek Church. Francis decides to go and preach to the mass of ignorant Saracens because Italy is full of doctors. Accepting in advance the risk of martyrdom, he hastens to Damietta. At the risk of his life, he crosses an arm of the Nile in a small boat. He is severely ill-treated by the Saracens, but his moral force compels the admiration of all. (Nevertheless he suffers not so much martyrdom as cruel harrassment by an enemy.) The Sultan receives him with kindness and pomp, but the only gift Francis will accept is the priceless present of simply being heard. The Sultan therefore summons his philosophers. Francis gives them a formal lecture in syllogisms on all the articles of the Christian faith, beginning with the oneness of God, so condemning the perverse polytheistic school of Mohammed (!). The Sultan and the philosophers are shaken. No-one dares to contradict Francis, and he delivers several further philosophical lectures of the same type. Being unable on his own to convert 'a multitude of Persians' for want of ministers to help him, Francis finds himself obliged to abandon the work he has begun so well and return to the crusaders' camp.

These are a few pieces of evidence from sources outside the order which stress the doctoral aspect of the encounter between Francis and the Sultan: the object is to fight Islam, not with arms, but by 'straight argument'. This is said to be the risk Francis took.

(b) The Brethren of the Order

The messages of the legends belonging to the order sound quite a different note. Here the encounter with Islam acquires its meaning as part of Francis' destiny. But what is that meaning?

Francis' first hagiographer in the order, *Thomas of Celano*, wrote his *Vita I* as early as 1228 on the order of the pope. Francis the merchant dreams of being a knight, but his initial conversion consists in transforming this worldly chivalry into a spiritual crusade unheard of in his day. How tempting it would be thus to present the meeting of Francis and the Sultan in a context of the sublimation of the Crusade. Nothing of the sort! *The encounter with Islam is connected with the desire for martyrdom which consumed Francis after his conversion*; it is no more than an episode in a story with deeper roots. Had not Francis already voluntarily risked martyrdom three times in his ambition to preach repentance and Christian faith to the Saracens? More than any ecstasy, martyrdom is the only true short-cut to Christ. On his third attempt, Francis tried to reach the Miramamolin of Morocco by way of Spain: drunk with the Spirit, he tore along the road, leaving his companion behind, eager to arrive. God intervened directly to stop him by striking him with an illness. Finally, on the fourth occasion, when he took ship for Damietta, it was to meet the Sultan. The war was at its height, day after day, 'between the Christians and the pagans'. On reaching the Saracen camp, Francis first endured a minor martyrdom, which he bore stoically. Finally he reached the Sultan's presence and fearlessly expounded, with no attempt to soften it, the Christian message. The author stresses the contrast between the hostility of the entourage and the Sultan's kindness. Francis has to answer those who insult the Christian faith. Many of the courtiers attack the saint with hostile intentions and a spirit of contradiction. The Sultan alone is the exception. He calms his entourage and seeks to honour Francis as much as he can and perhaps to test him by tempting him with presents. Francis despises all. Speechless, the Sultan henceforth looks on Francis as a man who quite definitely is like no-one else: overwhelmed, he listens with added attention and sympathy . . . . The story ends with the mystery; we know nothing more! The author concludes that the attempt to find martyrdom has ended in another failure . . . . It seems that the mysterious answer to Francis' prayer is postponed. But did not this failure imply the dawn of a timid hope? The story of Francis' encounter with Islam can be told with the Crusade relegated from now on to a footnote.

But the converse is also true, because Francis' relations with the Crusade at Damietta can be described without reference to his personal encounter with the Sultan. This is exactly what happened to Thomas of Celano in his *Vita II*, where he corrects the general outlook of the *Vita I*. Still carried away by his desire for martyrdom, Francis arrives at the Crusader camp, but this time it is from the crusaders that the threat of persecution, or at least of insult, comes. Francis wants to forbid the war. He takes the risk of haranguing the army, predicting failure. He is taken for a fool! In the event the fighting ended in disaster. Nevertheless, the author still does not see Francis' intervention as a condemnation of the Crusade, but simply a warning to the leaders of the army: a war is only holy if it is inspired by the Spirit of God and not by the insolence of men relying on their own strength! And the visit to the Sultan can only be passed over in silence.

The most elaborate account is *St Bonaventure's*. Normally Bonaventure does not condemn the idea of the Crusade; he was even to send Friars to it! Moreover, he had little love for the Saracens, a 'herd of reprobates', 'fierce and barbarous of spirit', 'dreaming only of banquets'. Egypt and Babylon are symbols of the country under a curse which must be abandoned. But when Francis comes on the scene the language is transformed; the aggression draws in its claws.

In the narrative everything starts once more from the desire for martyrdom, but that has a totally different meaning from the one given to it by Thomas of Celano. Francis wants to make known the mystery of love of God the Trinity. His martyrdom is a returning of love to Christ through a willingness to die like him for those who persecute us and who remain always worthy of love because they are loved by God. In this decisive test one is transformed into him by that very love and one arouses a divine love in those for whom one sacrifices oneself. So, on the basis of Thomas of Celano's text, Bonaventure writes a new account of the famous interview.

The war between Saracens and Christians is pitiless. At Damietta it is impossible to leave either camp without risking death, and any Saracen who cuts off a Christian head receives a gold bezant. Francis is in no doubt! It is the hour of his martyrdom! The forward sentries of the Saracens beat him savagely, but at his request he and another friar are nevertheless brought into the Sultan's presence. The Sultan asks who accredits them: where are their letters of credence, their diplomatic authority? Francis replies that their business has nothing to do with the Crusade. 'No man, but God, has sent us across the seas to announce the Good News of the Truth.' Francis then preaches the Trinity, Christ the Saviour. No-one can refute him. The Sultan, won over by this fervour and boldness, listens to him willingly and begs him to stay.

Now comes the famous scene of the ordeal. 'If you and your people are willing to be converted to Christ, I shall gladly stay here with you for his love's sake. But if you still hesitate to repudiate the law of Mohammed, light a pyre. I shall mount it with your priests. Then you will know which faith is the holier and more certain.' Before the Sultan's hesitation to accept such a trial for his priests, the most senior of whom has just slipped away, Francis goes further. 'Promise that you and your people will become Christians if I go through the fire alone and come out unscathed. If I burn, attribute it simply to my sins.' The Sultan again refuses, fearing a popular rising, but he offers presents. Now it is Francis' turn to refuse; he is interested only in souls. Surprised, the Sultan, either being unwilling or not daring to go over to Christianity, then, for his own salvation, asks Francis to accept subsidies for the churches and poor Christians. Once more Francis vigorously refuses, suspecting the Sultan's piety. Thus, deprived of martyrdom and unable to do more for the conversion of this people, Francis departs.

A variety of accounts could be cited from brethren of the order, but we have an unparalleled piece of evidence from Arab sources, tracked down by the patient researches of Professor L. Massignon. An Arab author of the fifteenth century, Ibn-Al-Zayyat, testifies indirectly to Francis' visit through a reference to *Fakr-El-Din-Farsi*, a mystic who was influential in the Sultan's entourage. His tomb bore the epigraph, 'This man's virtue is known to all. His adventure with Al-Malik-Al-Kamil and what happened to him because of the monk, all that is very famous.' The identification with Francis seems beyond doubt; his journey had significance for our Moslem brothers too. So important was it that this man's dates would be known to all from his tomb solely through the reference to St Francis! The sage who slipped away from the ordeal out of disapproval of the Sultan is thus identified. And the mystic's person also seems to confirm that Francis was received by the Sultan as a religious messenger and not as a political ambassador, which connects this story with the biographies of the saint and not with the chronicles of the Crusades.

The *Leitmotiv* of this series is also constant whatever the variations. Francis' only reason for setting foot on the soil of Islam was his desire to offer his life as a holocaust for his Moslem brothers. With some help from legend, the Sultan even ends up being baptised!

A double conclusion arises out of this diversity. Just as the chroniclers who are outsiders to the order place Francis' encounter with Islam within the context of the Crusade, the brothers of the order tend equally to isolate it from the Crusade in order to interpret it with reference to an unquenchable desire for martyrdom. It is no longer an isolated incident, but a profound movement. But all these contrasting analyses converge at one crucial point; they clarify the historical status of the event. No doubt the journey may have given rise to legends, but it must be firmly stressed that in this precise case they are always listened to at the gates of history.

2. AN APPROACH TO THE FACTS

The two families of accounts present different versions, but do they not both show dead-ends and breaks? At the height of the siege of Damietta, the Sultan is unable to recognise Francis as a crusader and Francis does not recognise the Sultan as the persecutor of the faith he expected. Neither the perspective of the Crusade nor the perspective of martyrdom can do justice to this meeting, which certainly took place in conditions which confused the very participants.

That is why the accounts seem to waver in their own logic, because of the presuppositions of the narrators, unless there was an inconsistency in the hero himself! Since there is no room here to subject all the accounts to a critical analysis, let us see what picture of the facts we can obtain through each perspective.

(a) The perspective of the Crusade

In his youthful dreams Francis was obsessed by chivalry and even the Crusade, which aroused in him, not a thirst for sacrifice, but a universal ambition. Once converted, Francis still entertains apostolic ambitions on a world scale: from the start the mission to the infidels is virtually present in the initial fervour. But is it yet a Crusade?

In 1212 the victory of Las Navas over the Saracens in Spain confirmed Innocent III in his plan of launching a new Crusade to reform the Church. If the tomb of Christ were reconquered, Christianity would emerge from it as if resurrected! Council and Crusade were announced together the next year and preachers sent everywhere to plead the cause of the Holy Land. In 1215 the Council fixed the Crusade for 1217.

Now Francis' attitude appears strange, to say the least. His first missionary journey had nothing to do with the winning back of Spain from Islam, since he left for Syria a year before (1211). The word 'knight', never appears in his writings, still less 'crusader'. No biographer in the preceding accounts dared to present him as such. He never sent his friars as preachers of the Crusade (it was rather the latter who became friars!). Never does he have any sense of superiority to the 'infidel'; everything comes from the grace of God and if the 'infidel' had had the same grace as Francis he would have been more grateful. This is why Francis is everywhere no more than a 'friar minor'. Never does any term or allusion offensive to Islam appear in his writings, something very rare in his day, even among saints. Furthermore, both in Morocco and in Syria, Francis never played the role of 'military chaplain'. He went directly to see the enemy rulers, keeping above the Crusade and the Reconquista. Even more striking, after sending friars to Morocco and Syria long before the Crusade, we find him in the year of the Crusade itself, 1217, forbidding in the General Chapter the sending of any missionaries to prevent any ambiguity with Islam. The friars are sent only to Christian countries. When Cardinal

Hugolin traps him in Florence to forbid him to go to France, a new impulse towards the infidels awakens strongly in him, but as though to counter the Crusade. He had already obtained from Pope Honorius III (1216) the Portiuncula indulgence, which granted for nothing to poor pilgrims the same privileges as the crusaders! What cheek! And at the very moment that the pope gave his friars letters of protection to prevent their being annoyed further by the clergy, Francis chose to leave for Moslem territory with no other protection at the risk of martyrdom (1219). On reaching Damietta, Francis attempted to dissuade the crusaders from fighting and refused to take part in the attack. But the Crusade ignored him; it was the Sultan who was to listen to him!

It thus seems fully proven that Francis' action is the exact opposite of any Crusade mysticism. No sublimation is possible! Francis is not Bernard! And when Francis reached the Sultan no doubt was possible, as all the sources, almost in spite of themselves, confirm: Francis did not come to Islamic territory on behalf of the crusaders. So on whose behalf did he come?

(b) The perspective of martyrdom

When Francis learned of the martyrdom of the friars in Morocco, he was to exclaim first, 'At last I have five real friars minor!' But did not that risk being an insult to Islam? Francis did not want to risk any ambiguity. He wanted to be martyred, not as a crusader—that would have been too banal!—but as a Christian. He maintained that the Koran could not but put him to death for his Christian faith. But by accepting that death in confessing his faith Francis would prove its truth by the love he showed his murderers, even if they thought their actions gave glory to God. And like Jesus in that pardon he would destroy the wall of hatred. This seems to have been his missionary premise or prejudice. But is it defensible?

First observation. Francis really thought at the beginning that his martyrdom, if it occurred, would speak to Islam. It should be stressed that in general martyrdom is addressed more to the Church than to the killers and strengthens the faith of the community. And what is more, it must not be sought or provoked.

But to make martyrdom itself an act of missionary apostolate in all lucidity was something which was far from obvious. Francis' boldness lay in thinking that his martyrdom would speak more to Islam than to the Church. Against the extravagance of the Crusade, Islam required a radical witness which would be the radical opposite. Martyrdom is the conscientious objection raised against all those who support the intolerance of a holy war; it is an anti-crusade.

Second observation. The ill-treatment received by Francis at Damietta is almost passed over in silence by the authors from outside the order, but heavily stressed by the Franciscan chroniclers. The cruelty of the Saracens thus acts as a foil to the excellence of the hero and confers on him a semblance of martyrdom (and so even indirectly justifies the Crusade). But Francis is persecuted like any crusader as long as he is not identified as a Christian; on the other hand, once he is recognised as a Christian the tortures stop. So what he suffered he did not endure for the sake of his Christian faith. This is implicitly recognised by all the sources. And as long as the friars confess Christ without insulting Mohammed, they are never ill-treated. This is the basic pattern. The Sultan's friendliness did not come from any attraction exercised by the gospel, but was no more than a return to the purest essence of the Koran. Consequently—however paradoxical it may appear—the desire for martyrdom cannot strictly be fulfilled in Islam, so our sources say, in the case of a 'real Christian'.

Third observation. Francis at Damietta tried to force destiny, to anticipate the end in his impatience to get results at all costs. Normally martyrdom forces the believer into his own decision, but not necessarily others. Here it is the opposite. A sermon by St

Bonaventure, separated from the underlying text of Thomas of Celano's *Vita I*, seems to confirm this impression. Resolute and ready for anything, Francis preached the Christian faith. It was a confession of faith, a kerygma, rather than a catechesis. The Sultan readily listened to this man of fire, but without committing himself. Francis tried to force a decision. The Sultan retreated to the level of discussion. Francis bluntly refused: faith transcends reason, he argued, and reasons are worth anything only within faith. From that point all dialogue was impossible. It was now that Francis proposed the ordeal to tear the Sultan out of his hesitation. But this takes us out of the strict logic of martyrdom. We are no longer in mysticism, but in apologetics—a living argument presented by God. If Francis were burned, it would not be as a martyr, not as a confessor, but as a sinner. But what would have been his sin? Surely none other than to have risked the ordeal and tempted the Lord God? Though even that failure ought not to prevent the Sultan from believing anyway. The risk was dictated by love: testimony and test coincide. If Francis were burned by God in fire while all the time burning with love for the Sultan, could the Sultan still say, 'That has no value.' Is there anything more to be said?

If for Francis the ordeal was the absolute proof, how did the Sultan see it? Was it for Francis a way of making amends for the ordeal suggested in the past by Mohammed and refused by the Nestorians? Might he have heard of that at this time? But any such ordeal had subsequently been condemned by the Koran, and that was the reason for the sage's disappearance. And the meaning this time would not have been the same as for Mohammed. Francis had no hesitation for himself. Whatever the outcome, he was sure of himself. What he wanted was to drag the Sultan out of his hesitation, even if this meant provoking God himself!

Thus all the signs are that when he entered Moslem territory, Francis was not all that familiar with the religion he was confronting. Jordan de Giano's verdict was to be that it was not yet the time. But Francis was so sure of his faith, of his conviction, of his truth that it was impossible not to believe a witness who had just let himself be murdered to save his killer. But he had met a friend . . . .

3. FRANCIS' JUDGMENT

How should we judge this strange adventure which disconcerts the wise and prudent? We have Francis' own judgment, and even that is two-fold, including a self-criticism and a reconversion of his basic attitude. Once he had met Islam in such an immediate way, he was to emerge marked for ever in his thought and in his life.

(a) Self-criticism

Chapter XVII of the original Rule of 1221, on the sending out of missionaries, looks very much like a total reconsideration of Francis' own missionary behaviour. The primary focus of the Chapter is Islam, for it is in relation to 'the Saracens' that Francis defined a model attitude which could later be generalised 'to all other infidels'. This section had to be composed with particular care and prudence because the friars carried the text of the Rule with them wherever they went: one friar was to be martyred by the Saracens with the Rule in his hands. Nothing therefore could be written which might offend Islam. A sentence from the gospel sketches the outline of the chapter: 'I am sending you out like sheep among wolves. Therefore be as wise as serpents and innocent as doves.' Mission, prudence, simplicity, these are the key ideas.

The reference to sheep among wolves could not be offensive. Initial aggressiveness was inevitable in the political context of the time, and Islam knew it well. One ironic touch was provided by a tiny historical detail. After leaving the crusader camp Francis and his companion had just met two sheep before being attacked by the Saracens. There can be no mission without first running the evangelical risk. The idea was to live, not separately in a Christian colony, but among the Moslems: had not Francis indeed received a safe-conduct from the Sultan to remain in Egypt and visit the Holy Places? This missionary appeal is 'a vocation within a vocation'. The vocation of a friar minor is a life in obedience, but in the missionary appeal the minister can do no more than bow before the 'divine inspiration' which makes its demand on the friar. His power is thus reduced to neither commanding, nor still less to forbidding, but simply to authenticating, to discerning the Spirit. It is God who sends the friars as he once sent his prophets.

The prudence called for by Francis invited the friar to think carefully about his behaviour: he was left a choice according as the Lord might inspire him.

He could adopt an attitude of discretion and humility. The friars were to make a point of avoiding all disputation. The theological jousting of which Christians are so fond is specifically forbidden by the Koran. Francis condemns his own ordeal at Damietta, but also passes a severe judgment on the friars in Morocco, Tunisia and Egypt who had systematically provoked an argument which was often insulting of Islam and had led to persecution and martyrdom. This was no longer permitted. Later, while hearing the story of the Morocco martyrs, Francis ordered the reading to be stopped. Did he not secretly disown them? And we never find Francis arguing with a heretic.

The friars' aim above all should be to be subject to every creature for God's sake because they are Christians. Being subject might not mean hiring oneself out as a paid servant in a family and still less offering oneself as a prisoner for ransom in exchange for a crusader. The aim was a quality of religious presence, subject for the sake of God himself and ready to perform all the humblest services, like Brother Aegidius, who became an undertaker's assistant. This could not leave Islam indifferent: the believer is above all a 'subject' of God in peace, like Abraham, like Jesus the 'Servant' (as the Koran calls him), like Mohammed. And now the friar is voluntarily making himself subject to those who feel themselves excluded by Jews and Christians. Does that not connect at a deep level with the meaning of 'Islam'? For Francis *propter Deum*, 'for God's sake', was always the principal motive, adoration because God is God. The fundamental basis of the Franciscan attitude was henceforward to be service to the Moslem brethren in a spirit of adoration. Did Francis decide that he was too impatient for results when he was with the Sultan? Hadn't he left too soon and refused to undergo the apostolic kenosis? But, Francis adds, the friar must confess to Islam that this attitude is dictated by the Christian faith. Life is not enough. One needs the courage to bear witness simply (1 Pet. 4:16; 2:13). In that there is nothing that can offend Islam.

In exceptional cases the friar could also adopt a different attitude, but he had to be sure of God's will, of his own preaching and of his manner of presenting the message. The essential is to preach faith in the God of power and might (the divine attribute given special prominence in Islam). But this Almighty One is Father, Son and Spirit. It is not certain that this Trinitarian proclamation was offensive to Islam at this period, but there is a point at which it must be possible to indicate differences. However, our text contains no criticism of Islam and does not refer explicitly to the Roman Church, but to the Kingdom of God. Moreover, the mention of Christ being ashamed of those who were ashamed of him was nothing surprising to Islam, which proclaimed the second coming of Christ. Through the ordeal Francis had, as it were, attempted to anticipate this. From now on the friar, like the Moslem, would wait for the coming; now, in the present, he would confess the One who would later confess him.

And yet, prudent as he must always remain, the friar must also be simple. This simplicity is nothing other than remembering that he has given himself entirely to the

Lord and that he must be ready for anything (not a whisper of the word 'martyrdom'). But here again there are nuances everywhere. While it may be necessary to flee to another place, it is not said that one has to shake the dust off one's sandals in the face of the persecutor. And if it should prove necessary to endure death, the friar would endure it through love of Christ. He would answer with his own blood for this truth of the passion and death of Christ, which Islam had always challenged. The radical transformation of the missionary attitude is clear. Once Francis soared towards martyrdom. Now the friar sets off as a confessor of the faith in an attitude of service, reserve and humility. Martyrdom is now simply the extreme case. In the Rule of 1223 it is not even mentioned, while the attitude of deference and courtesy becomes an attitude characteristic of the friars throughout the world. The texts alone certainly bear the unmistakable sign of an exercise in self-criticism by Francis.

(b) A New Conversion

More and more after his self-criticism, Francis was to go on to make a deep reassessment of his ultimate spiritual attitudes.

Already he was beginning to express himself in slightly different ways from before. Very impressed by the Moslem custom of prostration at the call of the muezzin, he recommended his friars to follow suit. He seems also to have been grateful to Islam for its veneration of the Holy Sepulchre when it was threatened with destruction. The affirmation *Solus Deus, Deus Solus* constantly reappears as a reference to his mystery. Instead of preaching one God in three Persons, he worked his way towards the mystery of the three Persons united by love in one God whom no human being is worthy to name. God is what cannot be said. His good pleasure alone justifies everything. In this way Islam stimulated in Francis' spiritual life a resurgence of transcendence, but one which made him even more aware of the humble sublimity and the sublime humility of the Most High, Almighty and Good Lord.

But what was to become even more amazing was his reappraisal of his attitude to martyrdom, which is attested principally by the 'Leonine' sources (which have practically nothing to say about the meeting with the Sultan)! The martyrdom which Francis had set off to seek among the Saracens he was from now on to find among the friars: in illness, obedience and contradiction. Martyrdom at the hands of the Saracens might well have been less painful. Nevertheless, even if he had converted the Sultan, Francis now knew that perfect joy did not lie there! And his new habit of recalling the memory of Charlemagne, Roland and the paladins, though without saying, as St Bernard did, that they were martyrs, was not a sign of approval of the Crusade, but a way of giving himself courage and remaining in humility among his friars. And the man who had not been afraid to be burned, now begged his Brother Fire to cauterise him with gentleness.

Did the dash to martyrdom end in failure, in a nonsuit, in an ambiguous substitution? In Francis' unique destiny there finally appeared, like a divine judgment, a mysterious ordeal to prove that the saint's wild desire received a transcendent answer. At Alvernia, around 14 September 1224, Francis saw a crucified Seraph. The vision stunned him, but he now realised that it was not to be a martyrdom of the flesh, but the burning imprint of the Spirit, which would transform him into the One he loved. It was now that Francis' love produced his stigmata. The desire for martyrdom was fulfilled in a sublime and absolute way.

While all the Franciscan sources take it for granted that Francis found at Alvernia the martyrdom he sought at Damietta, it is more difficult to prove that when Francis received the stigmata he offered himself for Islam. (Readers are here referred to a hypothesis put forward with all reserve in *Francois, que disait-on toi?*) It is not unlikely that the authentic drawing made by Francis on the day after he received the stigmata represents an outline of the Holy Land with, inside it, the head of the Sultan confessing the Tau which is coming out of his mouth. It would be the most extraordinary judgment passed on the Crusade by Francis himself, that the Holy Places no longer belonged any more to the Christians than to Islam.

It is unnecessary to say that Francis was understood neither by the papacy nor by the friars, who continued blithely preaching the Crusade and insulting the religion of Mohammed. They were massacred. This tragic incomprehension was from now on part of Francis' new martyrdom.

According to a well-established tradition, the only gift Francis accepted from the Sultan was the muezzin's ivory horn with which he later called the Christian people to prayer. But in summoning 'the new people' in this way, as Brother Elias said, was he not also recalling the horn of Roncevalles, which prophetically sounded the last gasp of the Crusade in a sob.

Translated by Francis McDonagh

PART II

His Achievements

Michel Mollat

The Poverty of Francis:
A Christian and Social Option

1. FROM CHRIST TO THE POOR

THERE ARE some people who look on Francis of Assisi as a dreamy ecologist; others think of him as a sentimental revolutionary. It is always dangerous to transfer contemporary situations onto the circumstances of the past, and we should be very wary of isolating teaching from prior experience. Being immune from the charge of anachronism, the opinion of those who knew Francis could well be more authentic and more exact; they called him 'alter Christus', an impression of him as vigorously grafted onto the divine and, at the same time, profoundly incarnated in the humanity of his time, by a personal and deliberate choice: a Christian option, a social option.

Franciscan poverty has no other source and there is no need to seek elsewhere for the explanation of its nature and characteristics. Without going over the whole of Francis' life-story, merely reflecting on some of its episodes may suffice to discern the indissoluble complex of Christian roots and social insertion of poverty as he lived it. This close and necessary overlap involves none the less an evident priority of the Christian option over the social option. This priority is a prime value and a presupposition. This is not straining the story of Francis, nor interpreting it, but affirming it. The adherence to Christ which was his first step led him to conform to Him and involved the renunciation of himself and the world before returning, free, to the latter. Francis went first to Christ and through Him to the poor; then the poor drew him towards Him with them, in a sort of to and fro in which the human was inspired by the divine, Francis' essential aim.

2. THE SOURCES OF INSPIRATION FOR FRANCIS' OPTION IN FAVOUR OF THE POOR

It is not easy to detect any direct spiritual references for the spiritual option of Francis' poverty prior to the New Testament. The son of Pietro Bernardone had received the intellectual education, with a practical bias, which was usually given to the sons of Italian merchants around 1200. It certainly was not negligible, and the term 'idiota' which Francis humorously applied to himself should be taken with a pinch of salt. We know nothing certain about his knowledge of the Bible; it must originally have been the light luggage of those which later terminology in France called the 'simple people', i.e., the whole of the Christian people. Although doubtless light, this equipment was permeated with what the clerics had retained in their passage through the 'schools'. Perhaps Francis furthered his religious knowledge, but by what means? One would like to know the indirect paths via which he received the example of the penitential acceptance of dispossession and suffering on the part of Job or of the poor widow who received Elijah. Did he know of the spiritual poverty of the *anawin* of the old Law? At least the experiences of monastic and eremetical indifference to the world, deeply rooted in old traditions, were present enough to his generation for him to perceive, if not their sources, then at least their principles. Vallombrosa is not far from Assisi and the disciples of Romuald and Peter Damian could not have been less familiar to him than the sons of Saint Benedict, his neighbours at Mount Subasio. The poverty of the hermits of Grandmont, their renunciation of all possessions, the voluntary precariousness and unusual humility of their recourse to alms, was scarcely a century old. And from that time, drawing from the same sources, that current had continued to inspire more recent examples. Nourished just as much by strong biblical traditions as by canonical renewal, the environment in which Francis grew up could not have been unaware, by being either for or against, of the aspirations of someone like Joachim of Flora and, even more, of those of the trends of poverty which grew up at Huesca, at Milan and at Lyons. It has been said, and said again, not without reason, that the business travels of Francis' father, like those of his fellow-merchants, beyond the Alps, had carried back the extraordinary echo of the preachings of Peter Waldo, a layman, without mandate from the Church, but a passionate advocate of poverty. And Waldo claimed to be familiar with the whole Bible.

In fact, however—to remain on safe and proven ground—it is from the gospels and Acts that the spirituality of the laity, at the height of its expansion, essentially drew its inspiration. That was the true school which formed Francis. There is no need to recall yet again his constant reference to Jesus' appeal, exhorting his disciples to total renunciation, to separation from their families, to have no possessions, not even a change of clothing or a 'certain' dwelling; to the insecurity of daily food. From the ideal of the 'apostolic life' which had been restored to honour for a century, Francis upheld the total surrender to Providence. Francis' disciples discussed endlessly the nature of Christ's poverty, which should be imitated. It seems that for Francis this imitation consisted in conforming to the total availability of the Son of Man with regard to His Father. He did not introduce any intellectual consideration into this, since he went so far as to advise his companions against the satisfactions of study and warned them against what Gerson was later to call 'vain knowledge'. Is it therefore forbidden to the historian to think that, as Francis' 'scriptural' source was the gospel, it is to the continuous action of grace that he could attribute having access to that which neither flesh nor blood can teach and revelation of which is reserved to the humble. In fact, although one can safely include Francis among those whose dream for generations had been to 'follow Christ nakedly' (*Nudus nudum Christum sequi*), he cannot be considered solely as the fruit of a sort of spiritual determinism; his spirituality seems to result from an intuition received directly from Him whom he was seeking and intended to follow. This is how the dialogues with Christ on the Cross attributed to him in his biography should be interpreted. The contemplation of this Christ on the Cross in the Church of San Damiano lies at the very origin of his conversion. 'You are mad, Francis', Jesus is said to have told him one day, in a famous conversation. 'Not so much as you are, Lord', Francis apparently retorted. To sum up, the authentic motive of the spiritual option of poverty in Francis was to be free to follow the Master.

The imitation, the formula for which had by now been proposed as an ideal for the laity itself, was translated into the stigmata. There is no need here to discuss this, and summarise all the studies, including medical studies, devoted to the subject; nevertheless the object of Francis' impulse towards this imitation should be defined yet again. Francis never claimed to be the 'other Christ' that legend has made of him. Going back to the scriptural sources, one might wonder whether, deep down, Francis had not wanted rather to follow Christ than to imitate him. The person whom he wished to imitate was perhaps rather John the Baptist in his humble office of Forerunner. Not long before, Robert d'Arbrissel had invoked the same pattern. In his turn, Francis occupied the role of prophet or, to use the medieval term, of herald. He wanted to place himself in the last rank and, to be his companion, one had to agree to become a 'little brother'. This wish to serve in humility was expressed in Francis as much by his refusal to accede to the priesthood, which would have placed him in the front line among the auxiliaries of Christ, as by his constant submission to him who, more and more often in the time of Innocent III, was called *vicarius Christi*: the Pope.

3. THE PROMOTION OF A MOVEMENT OF LAYPEOPLE LIVING AMONG THE POOR

The marriage of Francis to Lady Poverty would therefore have had the original aim of preparing the poor to receive the Good News, of which they are the privileged heirs. In this way the social option is grafted onto the spiritual option.

The originality of this step must be appreciated. Generations of monks and hermits had already sought, in personal renunciation of property, the availability of grace and access to a transforming union with God. While Francis was a child, Peter of Blois was advising people to become 'a poor man among the poor', but this invitation was not new and was based on a profusion of experiments attempted to promote within the Church, in a non-clerical environment, a movement of laymen collectively and voluntarily living among the poor and in their situation. The preceding words are all carefully chosen: it was a question of the promotion, thus of an impulse, given to a movement, i.e., to a moving current, and not yet to an institution provided with definite statute. Francis shrank from this, not out of a spirit of contention and innovation, but out of a realism which is often denied him, and above all out of a very vivid perception of the nature of the evangelical message. Organisation had to come in its time, as a result of necessity. Before Francis, the practice of collective poverty had only given rise to short-lived attempts, which disappeared with their initiators or were absorbed into the existing ecclesiastical framework. The fate of the Order of Fontevrault, integrated into the traditional monastic structures after the death of Robert d'Arbrissel, was a recent and illustrious example of this type of 'recovery operation'. In spite of his esteem for the existing monastic orders, Francis never consented to annex his movement to them nor to adopt one of their rules. On the other hand, did Francis perceive the risk to which, in their turn, his disciples would be exposed? In this case he would have sensed, as not long since Saint Bernard had, when confronted with the fortune in landed property of the Cluniacs, the danger of assimilation into the environment one wishes to evangelise. Also he was able, like Saint Dominic when confronted with the setback to the Cistercian missions in Cathar country, to discern the unsuitability of former formulae to the solution of new problems. In the opposite sense, he seems to have understood the reasons for the setback to the initiatives, which were generous at bottom, but untimely, and perhaps also ill understood, of Peter Waldo; these doubtless lacked that grain of humour with which Francis was able to season his actions. And so it is easier to appreciate the unexpected—one might say: incomprehensible, without the intervention of the Holy Spirit—convergence of the idealistic impulse of the Poverello with the organising dynamism of Innocent III. In order on the one hand for this pope to have

C

consented, on behalf of Francis as of Dominic, to waive the prohibition recently formulated by the Fathers of the Fourth Lateran Council on any new religious rule and, for his part, for Francis to have agreed to give rules to his movement, there had to be on both sides the will to adapt the bringing of the Good News to the poor to new circumstances.

4. WHO WERE THESE POOR?

But who were these poor and what were those circumstances? In order to grasp their variety and extent, let us go to the end of St Francis' life; the approach of death offered him the possibility of a global vision of lived experience. The Rule of 1221 expresses, in an almost apocalyptic synthesis of human weaknesses and afflictions, a loving regard for 'all infants and little children, poor and rich, kings and princes, artisans, farmers, serfs and masters, all virgins, widows and married women, all children and adolescents, young and old, the hale and the sick, all peoples, races, tribes of all languages, all nations and all men of every region on earth'. In the background of such a tableau, one divines the social conditions and the problems of the first quarter of the thirteenth century, to which Francis was attentive, as to any 'signs of the times'.

Francis left out no one in the economy of salvation, which was open to all. For him, from the spiritual point of view every man is in some way poor. Material wealth and power are weaknesses; knowledge a source of pride, and its limits a risk of downfall; health a precarious situation. But love of the most deprived has as its basis a true theology of poverty, renewed in previous ages. Entirely based on Christ's care for the poor and, through Him, on the redemptive transformation of all suffering, the state of poverty is conceived, in theory at least, as a chance for glory offered to the poor for themselves and for their benefactors. Of the consequences of this first idea, one is the identification of the poor man with Jesus himself, whose image he is; another is the recognition of a place, a role, a status in the spiritual and social order, for the poor man, who is entrusted, beside those who pray, with a mission of atonement.

This is not to diminish the glory of Francis but to link up in this way his conception of poverty, at the social level and in the spiritual field, to the thinking of the two or three generations which preceded him and lived contemporaneously with him. The social, economic, political and intellectual changes, the development of which he was familiar with, had already completed in some essential points the principles we have just been discussing. Let us look in particular at two aspects for an understanding of Francis' attitude with regard to the poor. One is at the level of justice, the other at that of charity in the highest sense: love. Justice: already, those Fathers of the Church Chrysostom and Basil, the two Gregories (of Nyssa and Nazianzus), without forgetting the western one, Gregory the Great, had presented alms as a legal duty; but at the end of a line of thought set going by the ideas of Gerhoh of Reichersberg, Peter Lombard, Huguccio and, during the lifetime of Francis of Assisi, William of Auxerre, formulated the rights of the poor, including in them even the legitimacy of theft in cases of need. The Franciscan conception of the use of the goods of the world was to keep the idea which had thus provided the foundation for the canonical legitimation of the rights of the poor; invoking the *Lex Rhodia*, Richard the Englishman affirmed in effect that, in a situation of distress, all things should be in common and accessible to all. At that time, Francis was not yet fifteen years of age.

Around the same time, the promotion of the poor in Christian eyes took another step forward, in a direct line from the gospel. The pauper is not only, by virtue of juridical arguments, the privileged creditor of society. Prior to the vocation of the

Poverello, the meditations of Rupert of Deutz, for example, then those of Peter of Blois and Alain de Lille, reached an exceptional depth and subtlety. Thus germinated the plans which the Fourth Lateran Council was to change into directives given to confessors for the education of the conscience; and they did not confine themselves to a casuistry of alms, defining the nature and provenance of alms, the volume, the proportion of the levy on the property of the donor and the qualifications of the beneficiary. Peter the Cantor was heard to affirm: 'Do not consider the person of the pauper', and Peter of Blois proclaimed that alms should not have any limits placed on them. Finally, with a vigour that Rupert of Deutz's eloquence never attained, Raoul Ardent affirmed that alms must involve a certain degree of privation on the part of the giver. Using the expression *eleemosyna negotialis*, Raoul advocated a sort of pledged alms-giving by offering the example of the shoemaker who devotes the earnings of one day's work to the poor; all stations of society were exhorted to imitate this personalised gift, each according to his conscience. To give of oneself, if not oneself, without consideration of anyone or any limit: to achieve this perfection, one would have to be the Poverello. Being all to all, he responded to the problems of his time. The social option of his poverty is directed, entirely, as a reaction against all forms of abuse, more especially against those which, by injuring the most humble, through them reached Christ himself.

5. THE PRACTICAL ORIGINALITY OF FRANCIS

It was a far cry, around 1200, from the generosity of principles and the high-mindedness of meditation, to the living reality. Without doubt, from the middle of the twelfth century, the great flowering in spirituality among the laity themselves one hundred years earlier had engendered a kind of 'revolution of charity'. Pious bequests and the foundations of private individuals and parish communities developed a network of alms distribution and hospices which took over from monastic almonries. At the same time, the transfer to the afflicted of the name *pauperes Christi*, until then reserved to monks, was significant of a certain mental evolution. However, the benevolence thus accorded, not without a certain condescension, and often concealing repulsion or contempt, was directed by force of habit to the traditional poor: the needy, the infirm, the sick, children, widows, the elderly afflicted by physical or mental feebleness. But other misfortunes arose as a result of the changes in society. Doubtless Francis was not alone in his time in perceiving these miseries and in conceiving a broader definition of poverty. One of his admirers, Jacques de Vitry, a renowned preacher, who was bishop of Acre and a cardinal, considered as poor those who 'acquire their daily subsistence from the work of their hands, without anything remaining to them after they have eaten'. And for his part, the emulator of Francis, Dominic, declared as poor 'any man whose paucity of means places him at the mercy of the whole of society'. The contemporaries of the Poverello most attentive to human misery thus did not object either to workers earning an insufficient wage, nor to the workless, nor to the outcasts or those who had voluntarily withdrawn from society. Hence the originality of Francis consists less in an intellectual conception of poverty than in the manner in which he took up the challenges of his time to poverty. It would be too simple to say that he did not expect the poor man to come to apply to him, too simple too to affirm that he went towards him. The real innovation is to have placed himself side by side with the poor man and to have sought to rehabilitate him in his own eyes, by bringing him a message against poverty in the name of a victory over poverty. It was to proclaim the dignity of the poor man for himself, not only as an image of Jesus Christ but because Jesus loved him for himself. This explains the episode of the 'kissing of the leper'.

A gesture of love, that kiss given to the leper took up the challenge of the scornful opinion of mankind and gave them an example. The social option of poverty in Francis is made up of similar gestures. For to take up a challenge is not only an act of pride or contestation; it is also a provocation and a proposition, in short, fundamentally a positive action. Let us consider: son of a merchant of international standing, Francis knew better than anyone the possibilities of profit offered by the increase in monetary circulation; although the structures of commercial credit were still in their infancy, a young Italian bourgeois could perceive their effects, in particular the terrible excesses of usury which, although condemned by the Church, was nevertheless practised in disguised forms. These seductions of money Francis had at first benefited from, just as one can profit in the twentieth century from the consumer society. It is known how he took up the challenge, after having read the gospel censure on the evils of money, by stripping naked in the public square; scandalous behaviour for the son of a respectable family.

There were other challenges. The challenge of violence: here too Francis had tasted it. Having received from his father a beautiful suit of armour with which, like the knight any young bourgeois dreamed of becoming, he promised to fight in southern Italy, he gave it up and gave it away, to a desperately impoverished nobleman. The Poverello prohibited the bearing of arms to his companions. What he rejected most was the wrong use of things, hence his care to substitute peaceful conciliation for the use of arms, in particular in the urban rivalries of Italy, such as that between his own city and its neighbour, Perugia.

The challenge of power Francis knew not only in the form of force of arms, which was episodic in spite of its frequency, but in the daily abuses of patrician domination, fiscal pressures and denials of justice. Those who suffered under it were the peasants or artisans of his city and the surrounding countryside; and so he went to work with them, like them and with them, helping them to gather in their crops and working as a mason.

As regards the challenge to the public censure of outcasts, he measured its severity with regard to prostitutes, as also with regard to a younger generation as much unfortunate as idle, and often more rejected than wilfully rebellious; the pitiful adventure in 1212 of the 'Children's Crusade', abandoned in Sardinia by Genoese shipowners bent only on collecting the payment for their passage to the East, could justify Francis' vigilance. He channelled the generous impulses of the young towards the Lord by grouping them around him.

Another challenge: that to sensuality, to which Francis had at first succumbed. Soberness in dress, frugality in diet, the discomfort of precarious and changing lodging, prayer vigils and evangelising journeys were so many uncontrovertible responses.

Another challenge: that to knowledge; at a time when, at Bologna, Paris, Oxford and Salamanca, the nascent universities were encouraging a merging of the already vast knowledge of former schools with the profane acquisitions of ancient knowledge. To this, too, Francis said no; he refused, for himself and for his own, any other enrichment of the soul and spirit than that of the divine word. Better still, the Poverello also resisted the seductions of social promotion, even at clerical level, which could have procured him apostolic facilities. If he refused even this, it was not out of a systematic opposition to the ecclesial institution; he never rejected it nor condemned it, in spite of the inadequacies of the parish clergy and the want of care among the bishops, whom Innocent III accused of being 'dumb dogs who have forgotten how to bark'. Even priests personally unworthy kept in his eyes the sacred and definitive character of the priesthood. Francis respected the institutions and blamed the men, without condemning them. Attached body and soul to the Church, how did the Poverello dream of the Church? Not as a Church of the Pure since, idealist though he was, he knew humanity well; he saw in the Christian community a crowd of imperfect beings, all destined for sanctification and of whom the poor, more available because more unworldly, constituted the *avant-garde*. Thus another challenge was taken up, that of Cathar Manichaeism, of which Francis represented the antithesis.

6. IN THE WORLD BUT NOT OF IT

The poverty chosen and, if one might put it that way, cherished by Francis of Assisi is nowhere inspired by scorn, still less by a rejection of nature as impure. Quite the contrary. It is a pity that legend has overstressed Francis' sensitivity to nature. In more than one case, the sentimentality of *Fioretti* and of the iconography render insipid the real vigour, rare in the middle ages, of his admiration for the Creation. In singing of it, he fully celebrated the work of God and saw it no less fully destined for all mankind. Evil, which does not exist in itself, proceeds from the egoism of mankind and poverty from an inequality in the distribution of wealth.

Hence, for Francis there was no reason to retire from the human community. On the contrary; he wanted to be in the world, without being of the world. In this last challenge, all the others can be found. The major innovation in western society has been the rise of the cities. In the twelfth century, minds as remarkable as Rupert of Deutz and Saint Bernard had denounced them as sinks of all the vices: cupidity, pride, lechery, unbelief. What would they have said around 1200? At that time, in Paris, the parish priest of Neilly-sur-Marne, Foulque, was engaged in the rehabilitation of prostitutes; in Rome, Innocent III had founded the hospital of the Holy Spirit to take in foundlings; at Toulouse the Cathar heresy was raging, and at the fairs of Champagne, as in the Italian cities, usury wrought havoc. Francis' instructions were clear. He installed his disciples in the cities, but not in the centre of the cities. The first Franciscan communities were set up in the outskirts, where the poor lived. New times needed new solutions. The Benedictine monasteries had chosen to settle in the countryside, the only active place before the twelfth century. The city was spawned by the wealth flowing from trade and handicrafts; nearby, Francis installed his Mendicants, among the humble and the deprived, without neglecting the others. The option is clear. It conserves the permanent elements of gospel teaching and it responds to the signs of the times. Paradoxically perennial and changing, it is both Christian and social.

Nazareno Fabbretti

Francis, Evangelism and Popular Communities

WHEN FRANCIS OF ASSISI died in October 1226, his order no longer belonged to him. He, on the other hand, belonged wholly to the order, he was a definite 'property' of them who had agreed to be poor. The order had followed a logic which was ecclesiastical, devotional and triumphalist, whereas Francis had obeyed only his own faith and vision. He died bereft even of his own order, which had followed a road very different from the one he had laid down at the beginning. Francis' logic was evangelical and so it included 'failure' in human terms. In his *Letters to all the faithful* Francis himself had remarked: 'Everything that a man leaves in the world will perish.' (*Writings and Letters*)

However, neither an order, nor even a dream, died with the death of Francis. Although the order was quite different from how Francis had dreamed it, and the dream, which only he had proved capable of dreaming completely, remained at the mercy of the 'human order' and in the order of Utopia and prophecy, more than just a devout memory of Francis remained. His first biographers, especially Thomas of Celano and St Bonaventure gave a 'political' picture of him but never succeeded in destroying his message or falsifying its spirit. This was because Francis' own life was an unceasing act of faith in obedience to the Holy Spirit and to man. Eight centuries after Francis' birth, a genuine picture of him, even though an indirect one, can still be found in the two versions of the Rule, his letters, advice, prayers and praises. And it is also a picture of a family of *poor people*, 'friars minor', whom he wanted to be his companions and friends, rather than that they should form a true religious *order* with precise ecclesiastical and canonical connotations.

These writings, confirmed by the example of Francis' life, which Nicolas Beddiaev defines as 'the most important fact in the history of Christianity after the life of Jesus Christ himself' have been analysed, discussed, X-rayed like the remains of a saintly corpse, perhaps with the unconscious desire to reduce their challenge and importance, and especially their truth. In fact, in spite of all the casuistic surgery, private or pontifical, these rules and writings remain vivid evidence for Francis' adventure as a founder 'for all seasons'.

Even if these texts are not the ideal text that Francis wanted, they still remain a unique 'testament' in which obedience to the Holy Spirit and obedience to the institution of the Church are vigorously alive. They prove that Francis never even considered choosing any other rule than that of the gospel, the *literal* gospel. Francis was very jealous of these, his humble and strenuous 'tablets of the law'. He himself always made the necessary concessions to the hierarchy; he never allowed others to decide on this. Even when he was close to death he still had the energy and indignation necessary to defend a rule which was unlike any other. It was in the general chapter of 1219, when his friend and protector Cardinal Ugolino (the future Gregory IX who later made him part of the system by canonising him) advised him to allow himself to be guided sometimes by the 'learned brethren'. Francis shouted: 'Brothers, my brothers, God has called me to follow the way of simplicity and he has shown it to me. I don't want anybody to suggest other rules to me, not even the rule of St Augustine, or St Bernard or St Benedict. The Lord has revealed his will to me: I am to be a fool in the world. This is the science to which God wishes us to devote ourselves. He will confound by means of your own science and wisdom. I have faith in the Lord's commands, which he will use to punish you. Then you will return, willy-nilly, with great shame to your vocation.' (*The Legend of Perugia, 114*)

By the efforts of Giovanni of Naples, Elia and Matteo of Narni—supported by the majority of 'provincial ministers'—by 1223, the 'institutional transformation' of the order was complete: a *lay* order of *popular* extraction was already or already trying to be, a *clerical* order with solid convents, libraries, study centres and a growing number of 'learned brethren', prepared—in all sincerity and with genuine love—to 'guide' the blind Utopian upon the path of the real and the possible.

The friars minor were growing upwards rather than downwards and there was also an increase in differences of social class within the order, which only Francis, up till then, had been able to control and overcome. This was the state of affairs when Francis quitted the scene, subdued but not defeated, although he had been, to a large extent, betrayed. The most stimulating indications of his evangelical 'revolution' are all in the Rule and in his Testament. For 'Church reasons' Francis was obliged to accept reductions and attenuations. However, if we turn to it again today, in its wholeness without the diminutions, this *apostolic norm* leads us back both to the apostles and to the Third Advent, in which we are living now. The same popular and lay communities for which Francis set the example in his time, have rearisen today, in the different conditions and contexts of modern society. The 'base' has reassumed responsibility, without which all obedience is a burden and torment. And the base is again founded on 'lowliness', especially in the Third World, but also in the most contradictory and cruel deprivations in the so-called affluent countries.

These 'fraternities', the groups that have arisen spontaneously in this century—a typical example is that of Charles de Foucauld—do not have the hierarchical structure typical of the middle ages, which partly contributed to Francis' defeat. The experiment can be repeated, the same adventure braved. The proposed 'end of religious orders' can be seen fearlessly in this light. If we gather and unite all the experience of prophecy and service today, this will create a new situation capable of bringing about profound changes, but only if they are 'stripped' of all power and have the desire to serve that Francis and the first 'poor folk' had.

Francis rejected the classic structure of the Benedictine monastery—monks (*majores*) and brothers (*minores*)—but he strenuously kept both to Benedict's *ora* and *labora*: contemplation and action, viz., work. He added the *itinerant state* (instead of *stabilitas loci*), which connected them with the people and made the criterion of monasticism centrifugal instead of centripetal: instead of flight from the world it was a turning towards the world to serve it. Francis radicalised the poverty of the monks and guaranteed it with absolute poverty also on the communal level: they had no roof, walls, bed or stable work.

The concept and practice of obedience was also deepened and enlarged: only someone who is *minor*, the least, with nothing to defend, can obey without reserve. To the bishop of Assisi who could not understand how the friars minor could have nothing: Francis explained: 'Sir, if we had goods, we would have to defend them and we would need weapons to do it . . . .'

In the experience of Francis and his companions work occupied a fundamental and decisive place. Francis was undoubtedly influenced by the popular communities of his time. He worked hard like the *chassidim* (the equivalent of Christian 'minors') and was conscientious like the Waldensian *tessitores*. He was familiar with the condition of being an 'immigrant worker', as we would say nowadays: the friars minor of Assisi were also 'marginal'. But he chose this state in order to share the life of the poor in every way. He puts this plainly in the Rule: 'All the brothers shall work at an honest trade and any who do not know how to shall learn; they are to work "not out of greed for money but to overcome laziness and to contribute to the needs of the brothers and the poor". But they are never to be paid in money.' Francis makes alms an exercise in humility, both because it is part of *pietas*, that is prayer and contemplation, and because it may happen that 'the reward for labour is not sufficient'. Francis did not found an order of 'beggars' but an order of 'workers', although their work was always precarious because they were itinerant. Francis set the example of work: he nursed lepers, restored and looked after churches, helped with the sowing and the harvest. Egidius, his merry and sententious jester, did even more: he was a water seller, a nut gatherer, a peasant, a grave digger.

Francis was fully aware of the reasons why some of the schismatic and even heretical communities of his time left the Church. He shared their initial fury but always chose to try to reform the Church by example: firstly by not being greedy, not making the service of God an idolatry or the instrument of 'sacral' power. On orthodoxy he was implacable, even advocating imprisonment for ministers suspected of heresy. But in his *Letter to a Minister* (probably the strict Elias) he gives some of the highest evangelical teaching of all time, 'I will recognise', he writes, 'whether you love the Lord and me, his servant and yours, if you do this: if there is not one brother in the world, who has sinned as much as it is possible to sin, who looks into your eyes and goes away without your forgiveness, if he asks for it; and if he does not ask, you ask him, if he wishes to be forgiven.'

Francis welcomed and developed the idea of non-violence from the popular communities of his time. Because they had no houses, privileges or powers, the friars minor already proclaimed peace. They were forbidden to fight and the 'brothers and sisters of repentance', i.e., the 'Franciscan tertiaries' (the Franciscan seculars today) became the first great movement of conscientious objectors following two precepts which were unthinkable in the society of his time: they refused an oath of loyalty to temporal sovereigns and to bear arms. At the same time they were ordered, as were the friars 'to be subject to every human creature'. And this was also the duty of the friars who went among the Saracens.

Among the many devotions, which proliferated at the time even into superstitious practices, Francis picked out three favourites from the popular piety of the time—the manger, the Eucharist, the Cross—which permeated mystical theology, popular piety, poetry, literature and folklore.

When Francis was made a 'cleric' by Innocent III, together with his first twelve companions, he resolved the 'contradiction' of preaching the gospel, even though this preaching was reserved to bishops and the clergy and thus created a precedent which could act as an example both to the hierarchy and the people.

Another evangelical lesson taught by Francis was his total lack of the cult of 'numbers', as a sign of strength, efficiency and God's blessing. When at the chapter of 1221, he found himself standing in front of 5,000 brethren and heard about their devotion and also their disasters, he exclaimed: 'There are too many friars minor! Would the time would come when people complained that they saw too few of them, instead of meeting them at every step.' (*Mirror of Perfection*, 39) He instinctively placed his community in contact with the natural world, and he expressed and enjoyed its pleasures. In total innocence he rediscovered friendship with animals, the elements, sky and earth, water and fire, life and death. He wanted to make contact, even when faced with martyrdom and went 'outside the camp', *extra moenia*, and tried to be a brother to all. He did not attempt to convert anyone. In fact he never converted great sinners and the story of the wolf of Gubbio is a marvellous parable of a whole life as an offer of conversion to all wolf-men.

All this and more is still alive in the historical memory of Francis' experience and it can be brought to life again in the bare essence of his Rule and his Testament. Disappointed in a moment of crisis and conflict, Francis left the scene without issuing orders, but only after uttering passionate complaints. At the end, when he was nearly blind, he asked his vicar for a brother to accompany him and said: 'I've seen a blind man guided by a little dog. I don't want to be anything more than him.'

Francis was not the 'alter Christus' of the early biographies. He was a 'follower' of Christ and celebrated Christ's life and death with equal faith and passion. He was a true 'crusader'. He took up the cross in his own body on Mount Alvernia. To the new communities, 'free and faithful in Christ' he left the sign of a new way of expressing and living the specific mission of the apostles: to preach to re-emerging Islam.

What remains of Francis, what can grow from him eight centuries after his birth? Not all his brothers were unfaithful or treacherous. In an interview given to the writer in 1976 during the celebration of the 750th anniversary of the death of Francis, Father Constantine Koser, the minister general of the friars minor, declared: 'No, as far as human nature allows, the order as such has not betrayed St Francis.'

On the same occasion, Paul VI spoke to the whole Franciscan family in terms of sincere approbation: 'You are the students of the eternal gospel, freed in spirit for the primary quest for the Kingdom of God, which you have put first in your lives. You are blessed, preachers of the world of Christ, you are masters of Christian wisdom, you are models of the virtue of prayer and sacrifice which make the Church holy.' (From a message on a ribbon sent to Assisi on 29 September 1976.)

It is well known that in their missions which are outside the 'colonialist' structure, without fame or protection, the friars minor have faithfully lived the dream of their father and continued to give (and receive) the 'leper's kiss'. It is in fact especially in the Third World—geographical and social—that the friars today live closest to the passion and style of their origins. Apart from certain disgraceful idiocies—in Latin America: 'a friar minor can also be a banker', 'to strip oneself of every external sign of wealth from the desire to be like Christ who was poor seems to me to be an act of clowning which no intelligent man would ever do if he wanted to rule the Church'—there are groups within the order, especially those founded between 1960 and 1970, who live in small, spontaneous communities devoted to service and contemplation, outside the old structures. One group of friars minor (Cappuchins) in Chile lives a travelling life, going from house to house, working and preaching the gospel. Another group with a more strongly political line lives in the mountainous regions of Peru. The former editor of the periodical *Frères du Monde* is a member of this group. He writes: 'Our work is to bring to birth a free and responsible human being. The liberation of the poor is a key-word of the gospel. Much is talked about it but little is done. For me, this liberation is already resurrection.' Even in Italy, immediately after the Council, with the agreement of the hierarchy of the order, mini-communities were established, for study and work, and others which were itinerant and devoted mainly to helping the poor. But all these have now finished their experimental period and dissolved themselves or been dissolved by the authorities.

After the Second World War, the most genuine signs of a return to the spirit and method of Franciscan *fraternitas* appeared, and continue to appear, outside the structures of the various Franciscan families. The most authentic in rigour and spirit was undoubtedly that of the worker priests, who began in France under the leadership of Cardinal Suhard, Archbishop of Paris, and later spread to other countries in Europe, including Italy. Of course it had—and was suddenly accused of—'horizontalist' risks and the worker priest experiment was duly liquidated in the 1950s. It was the job of the nunzio Roncalli, the future Pope John XXIII, to carry out the decision of Pius XII. The worker priests did not live in isolation, but in small communities depending upon available work and contacts. They played a large part in trade unions and inevitably tended to choose Marxism as their instrument of socio-political analysis. At first they were tolerated, then they were suppressed so that they would not become a movement capable of offering themselves as an alternative to the established institutions. No consideration was given—even though they received many expressions of personal esteem—to the value of their becoming part of the people, their faith and work in a de-humanised world, in a country which Don Godin, one of their pioneers, defined as 'pagan with Christian superstitions'. M. D. Chénu in *Saint Thomas d'Aquin et la théologie* (Seuil 1959) traces this eloquent parallel: 'Taking a vow of poverty meant, in the thirteenth century, refusing categorically, institutionally, economically, the feudal régime of the Church, the 'benefices', the collection of tithes, even when sweetened by charitable and apostolic purposes. . . . The mendicant friars rejected feudalism just as today the *Mission de France* has broken its solidarity with capitalism: the same evangelical, not ideological, violence. It is the return to the gospel which requires the break with the collective superstructures, as well as with personal disorders.' (Worker priests in Italy were only officially recognised by the episcopate last March.)

After the First World War, Charles de Foucauld made another attempt, similar to a large extent, to that of Francis eight centuries earlier. It was not by chance that 'Brother Charles' went to live in the Third World of his time and today: Africa, the desert, the Sahara, a place to worship and to listen but also a place of human degradation and misery. The Little Brothers and the Little Sisters seem today like eloquent signs of the gospel: especially because they work with no other ambition than 'to be like them', that is like the least and the lowliest. Side by side with the traditional missions of the great religious orders, they live a life refusing housing and possessions, a life of work and contemplation, itinerant or at least dependent on where the work is, like the subproletariat of our time. Who is Francis and in what way does he survive as a model for people like this? Arturo Paoli tells us. (Paoli gave up responsibility for the De Foucauld brotherhood in Latin America and now lives six months in Venezuela in a 'radically Franciscan Carmel' and six months wandering among the poorest families and communities in the Brazilian Mato Grosso.)

'Francis', says Paoli, 'is our most congenial model, the one we try most to imitate. Because he did not proclaim poverty in the abstract, he proposed and lived in total identification with the world of the poor, the people, the *minores* and the lowliest of his time. He made a *choice of class*, even though he would never have accepted a *class struggle*. Francis, as Charles de Foucauld said, lived 'like them', he never wanted to share the power of the clergy, the priests. He did not want the girdle of the nobility, the shoes and purse of the bourgeoisie and merchants, the lawyer's ink-pot, the sword of the violent, or even the sword of justice. I think that the order of friars minor of the future should and could be a lay order.' (From an interview with the author.)

Also strenuously Franciscan, although purposely detached from any socio-political reference, is the work of Mother Teresa of Calcutta and her Missionaries of Charity, who have now spread throughout India, the world and especially the Third World, and are received with somewhat the same wonder and joy as the friars minor in the thirteenth century. Mother Teresa, who won the Nobel Peace Prize in 1979, is a sort of female Francis of our time. She says: 'Rather than a master, Francis is for me and my sisters an example of total dedication to God through Christ and his poor. Francis' teaching consists of being in love with Jesus Christ, his example lies in his having continually put this teaching into practice. There is no doubt that if Francis were to return (a pure hypothesis), he would serve the poor as I am trying to do. He would do it not just with words, but especially by throwing his heart into it and doing what the Spirit of the Lord told him to do. His example is still valid. Love is always new, just as the poor are always new, as are the lepers, the excluded, those without bread or hope. He has always stimulated and comforted me. My sisters and I chose the poor completely freely: it was the same choice that Francis made.'

Another experiment analogous to the original Franciscan one, was the brotherhood of the Falegname Companions of Jesus, founded at Nazareth during Vatican II by the worker priest Paul Gauthier and his sister in religion, Marie Thérèse. They followed Benedict's rule of *pray and work* and Francis' wandering life, even in dramatic circumstances during the last three wars between Israel and the Arab countries. Gauthier's particular aim is to build houses for the homeless, organise them into co-operatives and defend them as much as possible from institutionalised or improvised theft in their tragic and precarious conditions.

There are also other, less specialised houses in France and Italy; they are communal in character from the grouping together of either natural or adoptive families and their work is exclusively or primarily agricultural. In France there is the Arc of Giuseppe Lanza del Vasto, a disciple of Christ and Ghandi, a brother of Francis in non-violence as a rule of life. In Italy there is a similar community, with some specific differences, that of Nomadelfia, the 'city where the rule is brotherhood'. Feared, persecuted and dispersed in the 1950s, Nomadelfia was restored under John XXIII and now lives at Rosellana near Grosseto. From 4,000 its numbers have been reduced to 300 but they are trying to attain economic autonomy without denying their original inspiration. Cardinal Ildefonso Schuster, Archbishop of Milan, gave the war orphans to their adoptive mothers in the Cathedral in 1950, saying: 'This, brothers, is the gospel. All the rest is just the frame.' The founder of Nomadelfia, Don Zeno Saltini and the founder of the Arc, Giuseppe Lanza del Vasto, both died quite close together in December and January.

What tensions were there between the traditional structures, only partly updated in their constitutions during the general chapters of 1967, '71 and '73, of the friars minor and these attempts at a real 're-founding' of Franciscan brotherhood? The new energy is irrepressible. But for the moment it is only here and there. There are many friars who cannot accept, who are afraid of 'restoration', 'evolution' and 'modernising'. Of course these isolated instances of revival are not sufficient to give such a problematic and contradictory order the daring to take the brave steps necessary and possible today more than ever before to return to its original coherence.

Neither an explicit choice of poverty and lowliness nor a more precise definition of the role of the order is lacking. Father Constantine Koser said before the general chapter at Medellín in 1971: 'To put it with brutal frankness: the world has the impression that St Francis is a man with modern attitudes, whereas the Franciscan brothers of today are old fashioned.' Among the other articles the chapter approved the following (112) on a return to free labour desired by Francis: 'The brothers are prepared to give their services, even without pay, to help the poor and needy.' And also (113): 'The brothers, both together and individually, are prepared to accept any work and especially the serving of the needy.' And (114): 'The brothers are to take part with all men of good will in charitable enterprises of social help and international solidarity.' In the chapters and documents the term 'justice' appears more rarely. This is because in Latin America and the whole Third World, the exploitation of the poor by dictatorships and multinationals forces the question to be raised: should the brothers be just a presence or should they take part in the struggle? Were he here today, would Francis stand for presence alone, as he did in his own time? His visit to the Sultan makes us think that the answer is yes. But the Sultan was not a Christian, and so he was evangelisable, at least in friendship. It was with the crusaders that Francis failed most dismally in his mission. Because the Crusades were only a sacralised expression of the Church in power.

With all that is spontaneous and congenial to Francis in nearly all the popular communities of our times, is it still useful that there should be many friars minor, that there should be a number adequate to the needs of today all under the label of the great Franciscan family? Or isn't it, as Francis would say, 'the Holy Spirit who is the general minister of the order and descends equally on the poor and the simple' who chooses the real Franciscan where he thinks best? Number was exorcised by Francis himself, eight centuries ago, as a temptation and a risk. In this too, he remains an example and a project for the future. Might it not be these new lay, popular communities, within or outside the confines of the Rule of Francis, who could offer a lay version of new Christian community with adult faith in our secularised age?

Translated by Dinah Livingstone

Théophile Desbonnets

The Franciscan Reading of the Scriptures

'THE FRANCISCAN reading of the Scriptures': the wording of the subject which has been proposed to me causes me some perplexity. Does it mean that there is a norm—or at least a model—which would allow us to bestow the epithet 'Franciscan' on a particular reading of the Scriptures and to refuse it to another? My whole being revolts against the idea that such questions as this should be involved. When Francis wrote to Brother Leo: 'Whatever way seems best to you of pleasing the Lord God and following in his steps, you must adopt . . .', he was promulgating for his brethren a charter of liberty, which is none other than the liberty of the children of God. As a result, if the expression 'Franciscan' reading of the Scriptures' means anything, it can only be this: reading of the Scriptures by a friar minor. For the Franciscan charisma is not located in the past: if it exists, it is always in the present, at a particular moment, yesterday or today.

Shall we then be condemned to describe a multiplicity of readings in which, even at its most superficial level, the fraternity which joins those who have sought to follow in the steps of Christ according to Francis' example would dissolve? To answer that question it would be necessary to examine the works of a great number of friars minor (or at least of the most representative of them) who were theologians, exegetists, writers on spiritual matters or preachers, in order to ascertain whether these works reveal enough common features to define experimentally a 'Franciscan' species within the genus 'readings of the Scriptures'. In other words, do Bonaventure, Duns Scotus, Nicholas of Lyre, Bernardine of Siena have something in common in their way of reading the Scriptures? Such a piece of research has not yet, to my knowledge, been attempted: it may indeed be thought that it would rather demonstrate the fact that each of these authors was above all conditioned by the demands of his own particular discipline.

Yet, since I claim, as all Franciscans claim, to refer back to Francis as our authority, perhaps I may be allowed to describe his own relationship to the Scriptures and thus show what a Franciscan reading of the Scriptures means. In reality, I shall be describing the way in which, today, I imagine this relationship through the reading of the medieval sources. A limitation will be imposed on the excesses of my imagination, since I cannot make these sources say whatever I please. I must, nevertheless, as an historian, criticise them, since it is so obvious that the tendency to enlist Francis for some partisan purpose,

37

or to embalm him in a condition of anodine neutrality, has often been a factor in the composition of these texts.

1. FRANCIS WAS A LAYMAN

When Francis, impelled by grace, began his spiritual journey, he was a layman in the eyes of Canon Law. This reality, which I presume no-one can deny, meant that two barriers were erected between the Scriptures and himself: a barrier of language, and that of the book itself.[1]

(a) The barrier of the Book

Laymen did not have at their disposal the book containing the Scriptures. The price of such a book was in itself a sufficient reason for most of the clergy not to possess their own copy either: a Bible cost approximately as much as a horse! Francis would doubtless have had the money to buy one, for instance after having sold his own horse at Foligno, but he did not do so. More important than the price in deterring people from possessing the Bible were certain disciplinary measures imposed by the Church. Even if, in 1199, Innocent III's judgment in the case of the laymen of Metz who had had several books of the Bible translated into French was full of subtlety and basically very sympathetic, it is nevertheless evident that, for him, 'the depths of the holy Scriptures' were so profound as to prevent laymen from attaining to them: it was to the clergy only that this gift was given. In 1229 the Synod of Toulouse was to declare that 'laymen are not permitted to have in their possession the books of the Old and New Testaments, except for the Psalter, the breviary and the Hours of the Virgin; possession of these books translated into the vulgar tongue is most strictly prohibited'.

The precise extent of the significance of these documents (or of similar ones), in terms of space and time, may be subject to debate. In particular, on the basis of documents concerning Metz or Toulouse it is not possible to deduce with certainty the situation which may have existed in Assisi. Nevertheless, such measures, combined with the frequently reiterated separation of clergy and laity, ultimately had the effect of implanting in men's minds the conviction that the liturgical books (of which the Bible was one) were something reserved for the clergy, their property, in some sense.[2]

(b) The barrier of language

The other barrier erected between Francis and the Bible was that of language. Francis had a perfect command of his native language: the *Canticle of the Creatures* is evidence of this. His biographers readily emphasise the fact that 'he was fond of expressing himself in French, although he did not speak it very well'.[3] Yet none of them tells us that he had a good knowledge of Latin. On the contrary, in his chronicle Thomas of Eccleston speaks of a letter 'written in poor Latin', which is confirmed by the text, marred by Italianisms, of the *Letter to Brother Leo*, one of the two manuscripts by Francis which we possess.

Of course, this does not mean that he was totally ignorant of Latin. It may be pointed out that, as was common practice at that time, it was probably from the Psalter that he learned to read and that during that process he may well have learned it by heart. However, learning to read by means of the Psalter is not the same as having a knowledge of Latin. For that it would have been necessary to use it regularly, something for which

Francis found no opportunity either in the commercial world or in the merry band of young men of whom he was the leader. It may also be pointed out that the Romance languages became separated from Latin at different periods and that this happened relatively late in the case of Italy (the twelfth century), so that there must have been a period in which Latin, although no longer spoken, was still understood.

(c) The necessary mediation of the priest

Did barriers really exist between Francis and the Scriptures? It is debatable. But what his biographers do show us is that he did come up against them. The case is particularly clear when we consider two episodes at the time when the Order was coming to birth. The first took place at Santa Maria degli Angeli on 24 February 1208; four biographers narrate it in terms which are substantially the same. Here is Julian of Speyer's account:

'The blessed Francis, at the time when he had just completed the repairs to the three churches of which we have spoken, still wore a hermit's garb: he would walk, holding a staff in his hand, with sandals on his feet and a leather belt around his waist. One day, whilst mass was being celebrated, he heard the words which Christ had said to his disciples when sending them out to preach, that they should have no gold or silver, that they should take with them on their journey neither bag nor purse, nor staff, nor bread, that they should not have sandals or two tunics. Shortly afterwards, having understood these words more fully, thanks to the priest himself, he was filled with unspeakable joy: "This", he said, "is exactly what I am looking for, this is what I desire from the bottom of my heart".'[4]

We shall continue the study of this text later on. For the moment, let us try to establish more clearly the part played by the priest. Let us compare Julian's words '. . . having understood these words more fully, thanks to the priest himself . . .' with this canon of the Council of Tours, of 813, which commands bishops to translate their homilies 'into the common Romanic tongue . . . so that all may more readily comprehend what is said'.[5] The presence of the comparative (more fully, more readily) implies in both cases a rather vague ability to understand Latin but a need to remedy deficiencies by translating into the vulgar tongue: that, no doubt, is what the priest did for Francis. Did he add a gloss or a commentary to this? It is possible, but hardly very likely if we consider the fact that the practical consequences which Francis was to draw from the text were very far from the exegesis which was current at that time.

The vocation of Bernard of Quintavalle is the second event which must be examined. Less than two months after the preceding episode, Bernard revealed to Francis his desire to lead the same life as himself: a lengthy discussion followed. In the morning, Francis, Bernard and a third man named Peter went together to a church in order to discover whether their plan was in conformity with the will of God; they read in the missal the texts concerning renunciation of the world and decided that this would be their rule of life. From the *Legend of Perugia* (1241) to the *Little Flowers* (1390) we possess six accounts of these events, which are increasingly coloured by 'miraculous' elements the later they are. In the earliest we read that, once inside the church, they sought help from the parish priest: '"Sir", they said, "show us the Gospel of Our Lord Jesus Christ." The priest opened the book for them, for they were not yet able to read it well' (i.e., find their way about in it!). The *Legend of the Three Companions* confirms this: 'as they still lacked instruction, they did not know where to find the words of the Gospel concerning renunciation of the world.'[6]

The double barrier of language and of the book did, indeed, stand between Francis and the Scriptures, between the layman thirsting for the Word of God and the priest who had stewardship of it, and it was the latter who had the power to remove it, as he also had the power to consecrate the Eucharist. Francis himself recalls this fact in the *Letter to All the Faithful*: '. . . no-one can be saved, except by the sacred words and the blood of Our Lord Jesus Christ which the clergy speak, proclaim and administer. And they alone must administer them, and no-one else.'[7]

(d) Francis always remained a layman

Perhaps he himself believed that he was no longer a layman when, during the legal dispute between his father and himself, he refused the jurisdiction of the consuls in favour of that of the bishop: 'saying that he was no longer under the authority of the consuls for the good reason that he was the servant of the Most High God alone'; or else, later, when Cardinal John of S. Paul tonsured him, along with his eleven other friars, 'for he wished all twelve of them to be made clerics'; or else, later still, when he was ordained deacon, as in all probability he was. In reality, as Raoul Manselli has very pertinently pointed out, by the phrase from his *Testament*: 'when the Lord had given me brethren, no-one showed me what I ought to do . . .', Francis, 'in a calm tone, without any polemical intention and without revealing any trace of anti-clericalism, is recalling how distant the Church seemed to him when his plans were first taking shape'.[8] For the Roman Curia, Francis and his friars were hybrid creatures who could not be assigned to any category: was the fact of having received the tonsure sufficient to give them clerical status?

In any case, it was not sufficient to remove the barriers which stood between them and the Scriptures. The *Legend of Perugia*—in reality the work of his first companions, those who could say 'we who have been with him, we bear witness that . . .'—relates a significant episode in this connection. A poor woman, the mother of two friars minor, came to beg alms as she had not enough to live on in that particular year. Finally she was given, in order that she might sell it, the only thing of value which was to be found in the Portiuncula: a New Testament from which the friars read the lessons at Matins. And Thomas of Celano, who also relates this episode, concludes: 'It was thus that the first Testament which had ever belonged to the Order left it.' It is the date of this episode that should be noted: 'at the time when Peter Catani was Minister General', or between Pentecost, 1220, and 10 March 1221, when the Order was already over ten years old and when the 'Chapter of the Mats' had just gathered together 5,000 friars! At this period, then, Francis and his friars still had no easy access to the Scriptures. Raoul Manselli, commenting on this account, notes: '. . . in the mind of the narrator of this episode, the possession of this one solitary New Testament calls for an explanation', so little knowledge does he have of this early period of the Order. The episode of the New Testament of which Francis shared out the pages amongst his friars so that they could all study it without getting in each other's way, which Saint Bonaventure heard from an eye-witness, also relates to that same situation.[9]

There are instances of Francis' behaviour which can really only be explained in the light of that period. His insistence, revealed in various places in his writings, in more or less identical terms, on his wish to gather together in some worthy place the 'nomina et verba Domini scripta', the 'manuscripts which contain the names and the words of the Lord', refers back to a situation in which the difficulty of obtaining access to the books bestows on them a quasi-magical value. Similarly, the respect which he wished his followers to pay to theologians is no doubt partly motivated by the reverential awe of a layman for the man who possesses the right to handle the book and to mete out its content and its meaning.

2. HOW FRANCIS READ THE SCRIPTURES

Although he did not have the same ease of access to the Scriptures as we have—the Jerusalem Bible and the Traduction Œcuménique de la Bible had not yet disseminated them into every home—Francis did nevertheless encounter them and that encounter transformed his life. It was, indeed, something, so evident that it struck his contemporaries. Thomas of Celano, his first biographer, describes him as *novus evangelista* and Julian of Speyer, author of the liturgical Office, was to write in the fourth vesper anthem:[10]

> Francis did not transgress
> a jot or a tittle
> of the Gospel.

In place of this exact notation, the taste for the miraculous soon introduced the classic image which always comes to mind when the relationship of Francis to the gospel is evoked: Francis opens the book of the gospels at random, reads the first passage he sees and, immediately, puts it into practice, to the letter and without a gloss! In other words, and the question cannot be avoided, was Francis a 'fundamentalist'?

Let us first ignore the anachronism involved in attributing to Francis a tendency which, in that form, only originated in the nineteenth century, in American Protestantism. Let us keep in mind the fact that this kind of fundamentalism is characterised by a desire to interpret the text of the Bible literally, and that at first sight this is what Francis did. In reality the famous expression *sine glossa* is only found four times in the whole of the earliest Franciscan writings, and always in connection with the Rule. Twice in the *Testament* of Francis: 'I stipulate firmly . . . that no glosses are to be made either on the Rule or on these words (the *Testament*)' and 'just as the Lord caused me to speak and to write the Rule and these words purely and simply, so you also, simply and without a gloss, are to understand them.' The two other examples derive from a fairly late text, full of the miraculous element, in which Christ himself appears in order to undertake the defence of the Rule, saying: 'Francis! in the Rule, nothing is yours; everything in it comes from me. And this is how I wish this Rule to be observed: to the letter, to the letter, to the letter, and without a gloss, and without a gloss, and without a gloss!'[11]

The expression *ad litteram*, applied to the gospel, is also found only four times; never in Francis' own writings, always in the form of a biographer's comment. In Thomas of Celano it expresses astonishment or admiration in response to some new form of behaviour and prepares, let us note, the theme of the 'conformity of the life of Francis to that of Jesus Christ', which has its culmination a century and a half later in the monumental work of Bartholomew of Pisa. For the author of the *Legend of Perugia* the use of this expression is, in reality, a means of disparaging the state of the Order at the time when he is writing, by contrasting it with an idealised description of the early days when, precisely, the friars, following the example of Francis, followed the gospel 'to the letter'. In any case, if it was really necessary to show the relative quality of this alleged observance 'to the letter', it would be enough to re-read *Admonition* 7, in which Francis opposes 'the letter which kills and the spirit which gives life'.

As for the image of the book of the gospels opened at random, it is a naïve 'story-book picture' which cannot stand up to a detailed examination of the accounts we have of the event. When Francis, Bernard and Peter set off, early in the morning, for S. Nicholas' Church, they knew very well which texts they wished to read in order to find out whether their plan was in conformity with the will of God: they merely did not know where those texts were to be found. Their joyful exclamation: 'This is what we have

D

been wanting: this is what we have been seeking!' shows clearly that they had a precise plan in mind to which the gospel text simply gave clearer expression as, at that same moment, it justified it. This was also what had happened to Francis two months previously at the Portiuncula.

Before analysing the repercussions of the gospel in the mind of Francis, let us note the following commentary which may be found in various similar forms in the *Glossa Ordinaria*:

> 'In the holy Scripture, the true gold represents the wisdom of God and, in contrast, the false gold represents that earthly wisdom which is animal and diabolical. The false silver is the deceitful word; the false copper coins are the evil which has the appearance of good; the evil bag is the receptacle for ill-gotten gains. The two tunics symbolise duplicity; the sandals, which are made from the skins of dead animals, signify fraudulent execution of wills; and the staff denotes the excessive appetite for power.'

If the priest did give Francis a commentary on the gospel, it was probably in this kind of form. But it is obvious that Francis was quite unresponsive to such an allegorical or moralising reading of the gospel. Joseph Delteil has splendidly expressed the way in which, for Francis, the words of the gospel 'on that morning seemed strangely virginal and new, firm and compact, solidly built, literally unheard of before: that morning, *those words had a meaning*'.

The words were not, then, as in the traditional allegory, a mask worn by truth which could only be pierced by those on whom their knowledge had conferred the power to state their meaning. For Francis these were honest words, without a mask, which had a weight of meaning accessible to all. This is why, if the reading performed by Francis was not a literal reading, it may certainly be called a *realist reading*.

But let us come back to the text of Julian of Speyer:

> '"This is exactly what I am looking for! this is what I desire from the bottom of my heart!" Entrusting to his retentive memory all that he has just heard, he joyfully makes every effort to accomplish it. He rids himself immediately of everything of which he owns more than one and from then on he no longer uses either staff or sandals or purse or bag. He makes himself a tunic which is absolutely crude and contemptible, removes his leather belt and replaces it by a cord.'

Therefore Francis was nursing a plan within his mind, not yet clearly formulated. A plan which no doubt dated from the time when 'although he still dressed as a layman, he longed to find himself, unknown, in some town where he would take off his clothes, exchange them for those of a poor man and try to beg alms for the love of God', a dream which had been realised on his pilgrimage to Rome. A plan which had become clearer when he encountered the lepers: 'This is how the Lord gave me the grace to begin to do penance . . . the sight of the lepers was unbearable to me, but the Lord led me amongst them. . . .'[12] A plan which had its deepest roots in the gospel heard, Sunday by Sunday, by a layman who had understood it in its totality, a plan which, for that reason, had crystallised one fine day on reading the gospel. One of the components of this plan, a component which was to reappear throughout Francis' life, was no doubt a certain rejection of the social hierarchy, or at least of that produced by the society which he saw around him.

Let us now examine the way in which Francis read the passage from Matthew which he had just heard. The gospel said: 'Do not have two tunics!': to obey it 'to the letter' it would have been sufficient for him to have got rid of one, supposing that he possessed two to start with; he had no need to make himself another, 'absolutely crude and contemptible'. The gospel said: 'Do not take any coins in your purse (*zona*)'; it did not say: 'Have no leather belt (*corrigia*)', still less: 'Replace it by a cord (*funiculum*).' Now, what was the significance of the tunic Francis wore, or of the leather belt round his waist, other than to show that he took his place, or more exactly was given a place by others, in a clearly defined social category: in the eyes of everyone he was a hermit, and it is precisely with this observation that Julian of Speyer had begun his account.

By putting on this crude tunic, by tying its folds with a piece of cord as the peasants did, Francis was showing that he refused to be included in that clearly defined social category which was surrounded by a certain amount of esteem: the hermits. His plan implies, then, some desire for a marginal social status of which traces can be found in the first Rule: 'The friars should rejoice when they find themselves among people who are despised and of low rank, the poor and the lame, the sick, the lepers and the beggars of the streets.'[13]

Thus, Francis did not read the gospel 'to the letter' but 'beyond the letter', in other words, according to the spirit. When the time came to act, no-one, and perhaps not even the gospel, had commanded what he should do, for he was pursuing the realisation of his plan. Yet is was the Lord himself who had guided him: Francis had understood that in his moment of contemplation, for God always guides the believer by the hand.

3. HOW THE FIRST FRIARS READ THE SCRIPTURES

It may seem surprising that we have not, thus far, said a single word about the *Writings* of Saint Francis, which are, apparently, one of the places in which a Franciscan reading of the Scriptures may be defined. In fact, these *Writings* have already attracted abundant commentaries.[14] Most of these are often situated in the context of a framework of problems from which it is difficult to detach oneself, even though one may consider it obsolete: one in which the most important problem was to distinguish one's position from that once defended by Paul Sabatier. On the other hand, defining how far Francis may be considered to be the author of each of these writings is a difficult problem which is far too complex to be examined—essential though such an examination is before a serious study can be carried out—within the confines of this article. One simple example: Giordano of Giano writes: 'Seeing that Brother Caesar was learned in the Holy Scriptures, Francis entrusted him with the task of embellishing with gospel texts the Rule which he himself had drawn up in very simple terms.'[15] Should the exegesis of the Biblical quotations in the Rule be considered as if they represent the reading of Francis or of Caesar of Speyer?

Drawn up, step by step, by those who had decided to join with Francis to live the gospel, the Rule presents itself to us as a collective work, as recent studies have clearly shown; the part played by Francis in its composition is not separable from that of the other friars. Consequently, the quotations from the gospel which are to be found in it offer no more evidence concerning the reading of Caesar than that of Francis: in the end they represent the way in which the first brotherhood read the Scriptures, and that is what justifies the title of this article.

One must nevertheless give a special place to texts which belong exclusively to Francis, such as the *Testament* or the *Letter to Brother Leo*. We must merely note that they contain very few quotations or echoes of Scripture, perhaps because their subject-matter gave less occasion for such references. By contrast, as soon as a secretary is involved, as is manifestly the case in the *Letter to All the Friars*, written only shortly before the *Testament*, an appreciable number of quotations is found.

I feel that it is necessary, in passing, to make a comment about the method employed. In the various editions of the *Writings* of Francis—and especially in the latest, by the late lamented Father K. Esser—the identification of the Biblical quotations and allusions has been carried out by intensive use of the *Concordance*. This has often led to the identification of allusions which merely represent the emergence at the level of discourse of the Biblical element of the culture of the one who is writing. One should not, therefore, plunge incautiously (as is done all too often) into statistical calculations which are only based on the Scriptural Index.

Is something of the sensitivity to the Scriptures of Francis and the first friars conveyed to us through these texts? First of all there is their interest in the New Testament in its totality. Contrary to ready-made ideas which continue to be propagated, the Synoptics are not the only ones to be quoted. Indeed, certain texts even show a very markedly Johannine tonality. If the *Acts* are virtually absent, the *Epistles of Paul*, although relatively little quoted, are all represented (except of *Philemon*); the *Epistle of James* and *I Peter* are obviously privileged areas.

One may next note, with Thaddée Matura, that with only two exceptions all the gospel sayings 'which may be called *radical* because they force man to go back to the beginning and reorient himself at the very root of his being' are included in the two Rules. And these texts are 'understood and applied in their true sense, as modern exegesis seeks to reveal it. There is no misunderstanding or even adaptation'.[16]

Finally, let us gather together those texts which are cited so frequently as to show that they have preference, the ones which give its tonality to a spiritual teaching. It was around gospel themes gathered in this way, but interwoven and combined with other elements which were solidly rooted in a particular region and a particular period, that the life of Francis and the first friars was built.

No-one is good but God (Luke 18:19; quoted five times). *God is spirit, and those who worship him must worship in spirit and truth* (John 4:24; three quotations). *The letter kills, the spirit gives life* (2 Cor. 3:6). *It is the spirit that gives life, the flesh is of no avail: the words of the Lord are spirit and life* (John 6:63; 5 quotations). *Let us follow in Christ's steps* (1 Pet. 2:21; 5 quotations), *who though he was rich, for our sake became poor, so that by his poverty we might become rich* (2 Cor. 8:9; twice quoted). *Let us be like pilgrims and aliens in this world* (1 Pet. 2:11; twice quoted).

Whatever you wish that men would do to you, do so to them (Matt. 7:12; 6 quotations). *Let the greatest among you be like a lesser* (*minor* = friar minor) *and him who commands like one who serves* (*minister* = minister general or provincial) (Matt. 20:26 or Luke 22:26; 5 quotations). *Be subject to every human creature for the Lord's sake* (1 Pet. 2:13; twice quoted). *Say: peace be to this house!* (Luke 10:5; twice quoted).

CONCLUSION

Confronting the gospel which gives its rhythm to his life, Francis seems always to have remained the layman he was at the time of his first encounter with it. Like many merchants of his age, laymen who were as well educated as certain parish priests, he had the feeling that he could have direct access to the gospel, without accepting the barrier set up against him by the privileged status which the clergy had arrogated to themselves concerning the word of God. His culture, very different from that of clerics or monks, turned him away from the allegorical refinements which were then fashionable; it encouraged, on the contrary, a direct, realist grasp of the meaning contained by the words. Less than ten years later the clerics, having become the major element within the Order, were to begin again to read the Scriptures like clerics. It is none the less not a matter of indifference that Francis, their father, was a layman. All Franciscans, to varying degrees, inherit from him a concern to remain simple before the Book. Could this be what is meant by a 'Franciscan reading of the Scriptures'?

Translated by L. H. Ginn

Notes

1. All the medieval sources concerning Saint Francis have been collected in *Saint François d'Assise. Documents.* Ecrits et premières biographies rassemblés et présentés par les PP. Th. Desbonnets et D. Vorreux (Paris 1968). For the biblical culture of a medieval layman see Y. Congar *Jalons pour une théologie du laïcat* (Paris 1961) pp. 432-449; *I laici nella 'societas christiana' dei secoli XI e XII* (the third of the La Mendola weeks 1965), (Milan 1968); Various authors *The Bible and medieval culture* (Leuven 1979).

2. On Innocent III see *PL* 214, 695-699, 793. On the Synod of Toulouse, see Hefele-Leclercq *Histoire des Conciles* V p. 1498. On the separation of clerics and laity, see for example the famous words of the Decree of Gratian: 'Duo sunt genera christianorum', *Caus.* 12, 1, 7.

3. *Légende des Trois Compagnons* p. 10.

4. Julian of Speyer *Vita S. Francisci* p. 15, in *Analecta Franciscana* vol. X, p. 342.

5. Council of Tours (813) Canon 17. See Hefele-Leclercq *Histoire des Conciles* III p. 1143.

6. *Anonyme de Pérouse* p. 10; *Légende des Trois Compagnons* p. 28.

7. *Lettre à tous les fidèles* p. 34.

8. *Légende des Trois Compagnons* pp. 19, 52; *Testament* p. 14; Raoul Manselli *La Religion populaire au moyen âge* (Montreal and Paris 1975) p. 200.

9. *Légende de Pérouse* p. 56; Thomas de Celano *Vita II*, p. 91; Raoul Manselli *Nos qui cum eo fuimus, Contributo alla questione francescana* (Rome 1980) p. 144; Saint Bonaventura *Epistola de tribus questionibus* p. 10, *Opera omnia* vol. VIII p. 334.

10. Julian of Speyer *Officium S. Francisci*, in *Analecta Franciscana* vol. X p. 375.

11. *Testament* pp. 38-39; *Légende de Pérouse* p. 113.

12. *Légende des Trois Compagnons* p. 10; *Testament* p. 1.

13. *Première Règle* (Regula non bullata) chap. 9 v. 3.

14. In 1970, in his bibliographical essay 'Saint François et la Bible' (*Collectanea Franciscana* 40, 1970, pp. 365-437) Ignace Schlauri has listed 466 studies of which 76 are exclusively concerned with the *Writings* of S. Francis.

15. Giordano of Giano *Chronique* p. 15, a French translation appears in *Sur les Routes d'Europe au XIIIᵉ siècle* (Paris 1959) p. 34.

16. Thaddée Matura *Le Projet évangélique de François d'Assise aujourd'hui* (Paris 1977) pp. 46, 50.

PART III

His Relevance

Bertrand Duclos

'Francis, Image of Christ'

'HE CONSTANTLY carried Jesus in his heart, on his lips, in his ears, in his eyes, in his hands, Jesus everywhere.' This is how the first biographer of Francis of Assisi, Thomas of Celano, describes him. In fact, what is fundamental for Francis is 'following Christ', the desperate pursuit of his Lord.

Having said that, the difficulties begin, since the meaning of Francis' life has been variously interpreted. The same happened to the Poverello as happened to Christ and to his gospel, in the way in which Christians received them and put them into practice in their lives: according to some dominant theology or other, or according to a tradition which, coming from a place other than the Institution, has a different outlook and a different practice. But for Francis, as for Christ, there are things which cannot be 'appropriated', aspects which cannot be erased from their lives. 'Spirituality' cannot entirely replace the gospel, and 'naivety' of reading make one forget the necessary translation of the incarnate Word in time and history. Francis showed the countenance of his Lord inscribed in a world becoming the Kingdom. He believed that Jesus could only be found in the living flesh of men, at any historical moment. His eyes were open to what John XXIII called 'the signs of the times', those secular signs of salvation. Francis, through his incompromising practice of the gospel, demonstrated that the Son of Man is always present in the evolution of history. He took over this presence in an immediate way. He discovered that his Lord is poor, with the poor. That he 'made himself poor in this world' and that throughout his life he identified with all those who are poor, those who have been made poor, those who in some way are 'in a state of want'. And Francis made himself poor, 'rich as he was', in order to live by following the Lord wherever he was, wherever he spoke, wherever he acted.

'THE LITTLE AND THE GREAT'

In order to make his intention universally plain, Francis called his brothers 'Minores': the little ones, in every sense of the word. Little through their social situation in relation to the 'Majores'; little evangelical bearers of hope for a more human world. As they felt dependent on God, they also knew that that same God could not be with those who usurp 'the Kingdom, the Power and the Glory'. Little to those with whom—according to the gospel—Jesus identified (see Matt. 25:40), Francis had only one plan: to conform both to these little ones and to the Lord.

Thus it was that Francis, via his evangelical choices, made the face of Christ appear, lighting up history. With all his being he was bent on following the Lord, and this totality includes the historical side. Francis was not behind his time nor behind the changes it heralded. As a young man he doubtless took part in the taking of the Rocca, Duke Conrad's fortress at Assisi; he took part in the war against Perugia, and through his father he was aware of the development of trade and appetite for power of the emergent bourgeoisie. He knew the little world of the 'internal immigrants', those peasants who had broken free from feudal society and 'gone up' to the towns to find freedom and work. He knew the hopes and the material and moral poverty provoked by that growing urbanisation. He knew the little people of the workshops and cellars, needy artisans who decided to break out of their situation of being exploited by becoming a power through the constitution of brotherhoods, guilds and corporations. It was this experience of life that Francis surrendered to the Lord. The more so as he discovered in these little people, and in their aspirations, values which are not part of the gospel announced to the poor.

John XXIII cited as 'signs of the times' the great liberation movements of our age. Did not Francis perhaps understand what was changing in his society as 'signs of the times'? He discovered without any doubt that the gospel must become flesh where the Lord became flesh: among the poor. By evangelical instinct he understood that it is from this place of incarnation that one truly sees the love of God at work, and that any glossing over of this logic of Love is selling the Word short. He saw the poor working out new relations which witnessed to the possibility of escaping an order claiming to be sacred and eternal. For the hierarchical, vertical structures they substituted horizontal, fraternal relations—democratic, we would say. No more lords, but elected leaders. No more masters and servants, but brothers.

'TAKE HAPPINESS'

It is not a question here of making Francis out to be a social reformer and of projecting onto his attitude our own ways of analysing the socio-political reality. It is a matter of revealing that his way of following Jesus led him to the poor and that he discovered that the Word tallied with their aspirations for freedom and brotherhood. This human soil was favourable for planting the gospel. It was here that he should be, since Jesus had been here. For Francis it was doubtless clear that to live at the level of the Minores—even below them—was to continue in Jesus' steps. And to the end of his life, in spite of the pressures of the Institution, Francis was never to go back on this conforming to Christ.

Francis was not a political militant, but an evangelical militant, just as Jesus had been a militant of the Kingdom. Francis did not concern himself with 'taking power'. Just like Jesus, he wanted to 'take happiness' and point out to the men and women of his time the conditions of that grace. From the place where he situated himself, in contact with all the 'lepers'—whether in body or social condition—he included the immensity of the tenderness of God for that humanity imprisoned in non-existence. To join them was the first step in a rejection, a contestation, a demystification of wrongly sacralised power. It was the desire to create other relations, a desire so strong that it created an exemplary fraternity, 'according to the gospel', as 'the Lord himself revealed to me'.

Francis was not in the least naive. He knew that the Minores were also eaten up with the lust for power, possessions and domination. He knew because of his origins that the legitimate desire for liberation is mixed up with all sorts of appetites. The Minores had to be evangelised and the brothers of the fraternity had to be the leaven in the world of the poor in order for the latter not to become 'like the others'. It is not the poor who have the words of eternal life, but the only Lord who announces the Good News to them in order that they become, with those who join them, a new people, with new ways. In the image of Christ whose members they are called to become.

'WHOSOEVER WILL COME TO THE BROTHERS'

The fraternity of Francis was to be open to all in its composition. Middle-class people like Bernard, little people like Giles, nobles like Angelo: all have their place the moment they agree to follow the gospel announced to the poor. From the moment they count as little their knowledge, their nobility, their wealth and even their poverty, in order to know only the God of Jesus who makes his 'sun to shine on the good and the evil'. Francis does not make the poor a messianic class, for there is only one Messiah. But he is found only in the brotherly company which the poor dream of, who are always excluded from complete brotherhood.

That is perhaps Utopian, but it is a Utopia nourished by the gospel. And here was a group which set about living in a new way. The wealthy, clerks, nobles, little people, stepped beyond the bounds of their knowledge, their money, their arrogance, their resentment and their humiliation. To make oneself poor in order to follow Jesus was for all of them the grace of recognition of their equal dignity. For all men are equally loved, equally called to happiness: brothers. One can understand why Francis relentlessly hunted down the temptations of power in the brotherhood; his haughty mistrust of money and culture, because of the dominating use made of them by those who had them: 'One cannot serve God and mammon' and 'I bless you Father for having hidden the things of the kingdom from the scholars and the wicked, and to have revealed them to the little people'. Francis kept to that—uncompromisingly.

He called himself 'minister' of the fraternity and did not want to hear any talk of 'superior' or 'prior'. He wanted obedience to be reciprocal, for the brothers to be 'ministers of one another'. 'Minister' at that time was the name that artisans gave to their apprentices. It is also the name Jesus gave himself when washing the feet of his disciples. And so Francis became a contemporary embodiment of Jesus' attitude. To enter the brotherhood one had to accept that way of life, whatever one's social origin, rich or poor, cleric or layman, scholar or illiterate. This dealt a harsh blow to minds fashioned by the hierarchical ideology functioning just as much in the Church as in society.

This evangelical brotherhood had to reflect the tenderness of God for all those whom life maltreats. That is why Francis inserted in his Rule: 'Whosoever will come to the brothers, friend or foe, thief or brigand, let him be received with kindness.' The fact was that Francis wanted his brotherhood to be so open because it was his ambition to see the entire world converted into one brotherhood. He excluded no-one and addressed himself to all. He wanted to be a universal brother. He urged the world to acknowledge itself to be a developing human community, since salvation takes that path.

'THUS LOVE WILL BE LOVED'

Having his eyes wide open on the world around him, Francis saw that Love is jeered at, in the Church as in the city of men. Everywhere blood and tears, resentments and cruelties, extortions and injustice—and indeed right up to the tomb of Christ in Jerusalem, where Christians were set on making the Word of Love triumph by the sword. Francis mourned over this; it was the passion of his Lord continuing, and whose suffering he saw.

And so he set off, ceaselessly repeating an appeal for peace, an appeal for love. 'The Lord give you peace', he announced to all he met. Passers-by were astonished by this salutation. What did it matter! When 'they know what God is', they will receive this peace and their life will change. 'To know what God is?' For Francis he bore only one name: Love. The generator of peace: that is what should be lived, what should be preached, so that the evils of war and divisions between individuals and cities cease.

In the name of the essential Word, 'Love one another', Francis DARED. Two examples among many: the 'truce of God' which prohibited fighting on certain days and during certain periods, was not enough for him. Total and radical cessation of combat was necessary. To embody the beatitude of the peacemakers. Hence his brilliant idea of offering the possibility to those who entered the Third Order of escaping the feudal oath binding them to take up arms for their masters. A collective conscientious objection in the name of the only Lord! Hence also his behaviour before the Sultan at the time of the fifth Crusade. The Love which is God himself cannot be loved unless humans are converted to love. Concretely, personally, collectively.

One prayer attributed to Francis sums up his attitude well: 'Lord, make me an instrument of thy peace.' The serious doubts hovering over its authenticity cannot detract from the common belief that it could easily be a prayer by Francis. His image as an artisan of peace is fixed in the memories of generations and it is also known that this pacifist found his strength in the 'love of Love'.

'NON-VIOLENCE'

In a century of blood and the sword, Francis appeared as a man who has taken seriously the most paradoxical words of the gospel: 'Turn the other cheek' . . . 'conquer evil with good' . . . 'do not resist violence'. . . . He strove to apply these words—not without failure, certainly, for it is known that the 'gentle' Francis had terrible fits of anger: when he began to demolish the house of the brothers at Bologna, having first turned everyone out, including the sick; when he made a slandering brother eat dung, and when he chased an idle member, whom he called 'brother fly', out of the brotherhood, and so on. Francis was not non-violent out of impotence. If he refused to respond to violence by means of more violence, he also refused to cede to anything of his fidelity to the promised gospel. What is unjust is unjust and must stop, and when relations are strained they should be made brotherly.

In fact, Francis' non-violence springs from his wish to situate himself in the dynamics of peace of the gospel. He invented new situations where violence could no longer function. He did not make up any revolutionary theory on power, but constituted with his brothers a place without power. He did not propose a new economic order, but totally disregarded money. He did not attack the Institution of the Church, just applied himself to living the gospel. He placed himself 'differently', leaving to others the freedom to join him; to convert themselves, in other words. Eager for peace, by acting in this way he attested that this personal and collective peace puts in question the order which is established by means of violence—whether legal, secular or religious.

Without doubt, at this epoch in Christianity, this shift was revolutionary. Peace is possible if it is lived other than according to the permitted ways taught by the secular and ecclesiastical powers. Here again, Francis followed Jesus who, becaused he offered peace in love, so disturbed the holders of power and orthodoxy that he was killed on the Cross. We should strive towards a society without violence—that is what Jesus affirmed. And Francis pledged himself uncompromisingly to this course. Jesus' adventure ended on a gallows intended for runaway slaves, rebels, those who obstruct government and the full round of prayer. And Francis, at the end of his life, worn out by setbacks and desertions, betrayals and isolation, was to live that crucified death. What stronger image of Christ could be imagined?

THE STIGMATA

At the end of his life Francis saw the collapse of his project. The Rule he had composed, steeped in the gospel, had been 'lost', to be replaced by a canonically 'arranged' Rule. He understood that the game was humanly lost, just as the death of Christ had seemed to corroborate the judgment of the law-makers. But Francis knew that he was not mistaken. He knew that the road of the Incarnation is a road of contradictions, but that it is the only road. Hence that extraordinary episode at Greccio. He wanted 'to represent to himself the sufferings and discomforts that Jesus endured from childhood to save us'. All the Rules in the world with all their canonical astuteness can do nothing against the fact that God came, poor among the poor. That fact cannot be erased. And from 'Greccio-Bethlehem' the road led to 'Jerusalem where prophets are killed'.

At Alverna it was the murder of the Just which was recalled. Francis begged the Lord, 'I pray you to grant me two favours before I die: the first, that I may feel, as far as possible, the sorrow of your cruel Passion, and the second, that I may feel that same love with which you were inspired to endure death for us'. Tradition tells us that Francis henceforth bore the stigmata of the Crucified One. Francis conformed to Jesus of Nazareth! And here we have at the same time the confirmation that Francis did not mistake the path. The passion he assumed runs in a direct line from that of his Lord. He may have been rejected by his brothers, and his enterprise 'appropriated' by a myopic and short-winded Church, but Francis knew that he had not lost his life. Just as the Father was unable to bear the death of the Just, and resurrected Jesus, so Francis, betrayed by his own people, knew that he remained in the hands of God. He followed Jesus to the 'lepers' of the world and he bore with him and with them the stigmata of the inhuman violence of the world.

'BE THOU PRAISED, LORD'

'Crucified' for having wanted a more brotherly world, Francis was able to sing of the joy of that conformity to Jesus. And because he wanted to be able to say to all men: my brother, and to all women: my sister, he could also say 'my brother sun' and 'my sister water'. He saw a humanised world because Love is finally loved. This is to say symbolically that the reconciliation which makes humans brothers and sisters, because they recognise one another as children of the same Father, also includes nature. Salvation is cosmic, fruit of the love of Christ put into effect by men and women converted to love. Francis announced this at the very moment when what he had been trying to do in order to hasten the manifestation of the liberty of the children of God was attacked. The evangelical plan was substituted by a 'religious life'; the form of the gospel replaced by the monastic form; the relation of brotherly communion replaced by the hierarchical relation. Francis understood that the temptation of power had been yielded to—that power which causes the break-up of a relationship of equals. And so he only had enough strength left to announce, none the less, in his canticle, that the new earth was coming in which man, reconciled, with himself, with others, with nature, will experience reconciliation with his God. In advance he invites us to be amazed with him. For the moment, Francis might intensely live the Passion, but nevertheless his canticle has an aura of Galilee and the Promised Land. This earth, made peaceful, is certainly that towards which Francis marched.

And that is why he was transported by joy and why he believed the world should not be fled from. Here, contrary to that monastic spirituality which rejected the world as a place of perdition (it is characteristic that Francis was not afraid of women, who were traditionally regarded as instigators to sin), the Poverello loved this world. Everything was the occasion for him to praise God and we can read in his dazzled look his joy at being one of the creatures of the Lord. This is what the legends tell us, where we see the animals, too, told of the Good News: there was no longer any need to fear man, the great predator! For a new day had dawned: the day of the great cosmic fraternity. The day announced by Jesus and repeated by Francis.

FRANCIS QUESTIONS US

Replaced in this way in his own time, we can receive the witness of the Poverello as so many questions:

Who is this man, who believed so strongly in the possibility of living evangelically that he is still familiar to us today?

What is this Church which he trusted in and which broke the wings of his hope?

How is it that Francis' intuition, which brought him to live concretely with the poor and their liberation movement, was transformed into 'spirituality' which does not come to grips with changes in the world, if not into an ideology which stands surety for established disorders?

Why did his fraternity spend all its energies in 'religious' reforms instead of finding again its native soil: the world of the poor?

Why have only the sentimental, legendary, 'spiritual' sides of his story been kept, when Francis fully lived the changes of his time?

Why does his non-violence, lived as a system of Christianity, serve as an alibi when it is a question of solidarity with the struggles of the poor, in our secularised world where we have learned that more is at stake than good feelings, courtesy, even individual conversion in the transformation of structures?

Why is Francis' love of nature represented as amiable poetry when it is the expression of a prophetic design for a new world which is to be made to come to pass?

Why have his freedom and his way of ignoring obstacles become mere alignments with what happens?

Why has the Franciscan movement in its dominant expressions kept apart from history when what it refers to has ceaselessly recalled the realism of the Incarnation?

But other questions should also be asked:

Why in the Franciscan movement does reference to Francis pledge men and women to participate actively in the search for a new understanding of the faith for our time, by acting in solidarity with the liberation movements which are stirring in our world?

Why are men and women who are trying to be Franciscans to be found in those places where the 'signs of the times' are manifest?

Why, in communion with Francis' intuition, do they fight to give to the mission his view of the Incarnation, by living in sympathy with new cultural worlds?

Why, having learned 'perfect joy' from Francis, do they regard the world with a serenely fraternal eye?

Why are they people who keep their enthusiasm in spite of disillusions?

The image of Jesus of Nazareth, dead and resurrected, Francis is like him a symbol of contradiction. And nevertheless we believe that what he did is not ambiguous. He lived according to the 'gospel form', that which, in this era of Christianity, the movement of the poor is living.

It is for us to do the same, along the lines of the present-day aspirations of the historical movement of the poor, by offering that movement, because it has a right to it, the grace to bring about its liberation according to the gospel.

Anton Rotzetter

Mysticism and Literal Observance of the Gospel in Francis of Assisi

RESEARCH ON Francis of Assisi has always paid particular attention to his relationship to the Bible. A bibliography drawn up more than ten years ago already has 459 entries.[1] Since then many studies have appeared which in part provide us with quite new insights into Francis' understanding of Scripture.[2]

1. NEW INSIGHTS OF RESEARCH ON FRANCIS

These new insights are connected with research being given a new orientation. The old direction was marked by the priority given to the biographical sources which were then used to harmonise the writings[3] of St Francis. The new approach, on the other hand, places an independent value on the authentic work of the saint and gives it precedence.

Before tackling the actual subject-matter of this article I would like to summarise the results of this research.

(a) In essential points St Francis' understanding of Scripture differs from that of his biographers. The latter are familiar with the scientific methods of their time[4] and indulge in a form of symbolic exegesis in which no limits are placed to the imagination.[5] It is quite different with St Francis. He has no inkling of the accepted hermeneutical principles of his day. His exegesis is realistic and down-to-earth, his imaginative fantasy is tied to the actual words of Scripture.

(b) The thesis according to which Francis let himself be guided exclusively by the earthly Jesus of the synoptic tradition can no longer be sustained. The risen Christ of St John's gospel, Revelation and the Pauline epistles and the theology of 1 Peter are just as forceful and essential for him.[6]

(c) The view that Francis was the victim of a one-sided interpretation of the Bible is at least disputed today. If in his outstanding *Habilitation* thesis W. Egger talks of a 'one-sided selection, and indeed one made with reference to discipleship in poverty',[7] this is connected with the fact that, in keeping with the scope of his study, he is almost exclusively concerned with Mark 10:17-31. But a different conclusion is reached if one takes Jesus' sending out of the disciples (Matt. 10:1-42) as the starting-point of the

Franciscan life[8] and takes into consideration the other biblical passages that inspired Francis.[9] In this way Francis' understanding of Scripture is not eclectic but comprehensive.

(d) Francis' understanding of the Bible can also withstand the challenge of scientific exegesis.[10] One can only talk of exegetical errors if one arbitrarily gives the historical-critical method a privileged place. Thanks to more recent exegetical methods that have found their way into the interpretation of the Bible as a way of supplementing this, the surefootedness of Francis' understanding of the Bible can be emphasised.

(e) The literal observance of the gospel brought fundamentally new experiences for Francis and his brothers. These they equated with those that according to the collection of Jesus' *logia* befell Jesus and his disciples: lack of possessions and having nowhere to live. For sociological and psychological reasons the evangelical observance of these points soon led to a 'parallel' situation in which Francis participated in the experiences of Jesus and which in turn permitted conclusions about Jesus' experiences.[11]

(f) Despite the literalness with which Francis understood and followed the gospel as a prescription for conduct, his relationship to Scripture was nevertheless of a spiritual nature. On this he drew up something like a hermeneutical treatise,[12] the seventh admonition.[13] In this it becomes clear that the saint read the Bible on Johannine presuppositions.[14] Thus he was able to experience the words of Jesus as 'spirit and life' (John 6:63), a phrase which consequently became a central expression in the Franciscan vocabulary. W. Egger has identified the steps that make up this interpretation of Scripture and summarised them as follows: 'Outward respect of God's word; being prepared for spiritual conversion; inward poverty in the sight of God; putting God's word into effect (hence closeness to passages that demand action); the meaning of the Bible is to be found in action.[15]

This relation of 'spirit' and 'letter' must now be investigated more closely.

2. LITERAL OBSERVANCE OF THE GOSPEL

In his testament Francis considers two opposing possible ways of reading Scripture. On the one hand he urges the simple, honest and literal observance of the gospel; on the other he forbids his brothers to make use of any 'gloss'.[16] This needs looking at more closely.

The contrast we are dealing with here is subjected to mystification in the biographical literature. When some ministers provincial declined to accept the gospel-inspired Rule, the risen Christ took a hand. 'Francis', he said, 'nothing in the Rule comes from you; everything in it comes from me. I wish this Rule to be observed to the letter, to the letter, to the letter, without a gloss, without a gloss, without a gloss'.[17] Here we have projected on to God a passionate concern for the literal observance of the gospel and an equally passionate rejection of everything standing in the way of this immediate relation to the gospel.

What was emphasised about Francis himself was the way he was always concerned about the literal observance of the gospel.[18] Thus for example Matt. 6:34 ('Take no thought for the morrow') was taken seriously in a radical manner. The brothers did not follow the usual custom of putting their beans to soak in warm water the day before they were to be eaten, but only after matins on the day itself. Similarly they did not accept more alms than they could use on the day in question.[19] Such a radical understanding of Scripture has retained its provocative power until today.

Since the beginning of this century we have had, particularly among the Protestant churches, the phenomenon of 'fundamentalism'[20] or of the 'evangelical' movement[21] which have emerged with a similar understanding of Scripture. Bearing this in mind, and

E

making allowances for the unavoidable process of abbreviation, we can go on to present a more detailed picture of Francis' literal observance of the gospel.

3. OBJECTIFIED OR PERSONAL TRUTH

The starting-point for fundamentalism is belief in verbal inspiration. It is convinced that every detail of the form and content of Scripture is of divine origin. In this way divine truth is objectified in the words and sentences of holy Scripture. Hence it is always available and at one's disposal, a kind of thing which one can always refer to and appropriate.

The Franciscan view is diametrically opposed to this understanding of truth. As far as Francis is concerned the truth of holy Scripture is not simply to hand and available but has to be experienced in a comprehensive and personal context. It was at a service of worship that he experienced Jesus' sending out of the disciples as something that affected him and kindled his enthusiasm, as something in which his whole life was summed up.[22] Again, when Francis found his first two companions he went with them to church to submit themselves to the Scriptures, and did so within the context of prayer: 'Therefore, they besought God that he would show them his will the first time they opened the book. When their prayer was ended, blessed Francis, kneeling before the altar, took the closed book [and] opened it . . . .'[23] If we read the continuation of this passage we are struck by two further examples of prayer being emphasised. Reading Scripture thus stands in a personal field of relationships marked by dialogue. Francis himself connected the discovery of his way of life not with the text of passage of Scripture that was materially present but with a direct intervention 'of the Most High himself'.[24] The expression he used for this was *revelatio*. Generally in the story of his life Francis knows that he is always being guided by God, receiving gifts from God, being challenged by God. Practically every sentence in his testament underlines these personal categories within which holy Scripture is only the medium and never objectified truth. Hence, Francis often speaks of 'divine inspiration'[25] which clearly must affect the word of the Bible and which presupposes personal freedom as it does inward poverty and the ability to detach oneself from things. The seventh admonition that has already been mentioned talks of the fatal possibility of reading the Bible in an unspiritual and non-personal or fundamentalist way: 'A man has been killed by the letter when he wants to know quotations only so that people will think he is very learned and he can make money to give to his relatives and friends. A religious has been killed by the letter when he has no desire to follow the spirit of Sacred Scripture, but wants to know what it says only so that he can explain it to others.'[26]

4. PROHIBITIVE OR PERSONAL EXEGESIS

Thanks to its basic thesis of verbal inspiration, fundamentalism tends towards the view that the gospel is a kind of law by which human life is regulated in all its details.

The extent to which on this point too, Francis differed from fundamentalism is shown by an incident at the Chapter of Mats. Some brothers were not satisfied with the rule drawn up by Francis because it did not suit their legalistic outlook. As a result they wanted to draw on Benedict, Augustine and Bernard. These would show how one could 'live under a rule in this manner or that'.[27] Indignation and passion can be detected in St Francis' answer: 'My brothers, my brothers, God called me to walk in the way of humility and showed me the way of simplicity. I do not want to hear any mention of the rule of St Augustine, of St Bernard, or of St Benedict. The Lord has told me that he wanted to make a new fool of me in the world, and God does not want to lead us by any other knowledge than that. God will use your personal knowledge and your wisdom to confound you.'[28] Francis therefore stuck to his understanding of Scripture. He distanced himself from the legalistic interpretation of holy Scripture as was suggested to him as an alternative by a strong group within his community. Francis also opted for the non-legalistic free interpretation of the gospel when he was in the Holy Land and a brother brought him the news that his deputies had issued new regulations including new fasting laws. Francis was at table with a good piece of meat before him, and said to his companion: 'Let us then, in keeping with the gospel, eat what is set before us!'[29] The passage referred to here—Luke 10:8—is also to be found in the rule.[30]

These are not isolated incidents but indicate an attitude that Francis allowed to predominate at all stages of the rule's revision. Following both the biographical sources and the internal evidence of the text itself we can today say the following: Originally the rule of St Francis consisted of a few passages from the gospel, restricted to Jesus' sending out of the disciples, the sermon on the mount, and the story of the rich young man. To these were added a mere handful of prescriptions that were absolutely essential for a life in common. This primitive rule was then revised every few years: the brothers reflected on their experience and interpreted it spiritually in the light of the Bible; possible dangers to the Franciscan way of life were indicated; and the need that had newly arisen of finding the necessary regulations was met. With time this led to the emergence of a considerably longer text, the *Regula non bullata*, which for the most part consists of passages from the Bible and prayers with very few actual regulations. The fundamental aim of this text was then carried over into the *Regula bullata*, which became necessary because the need for a text that was more linear and more graspable grew too great. Nevertheless it is clear that for Francis himself this text is open to new experiences and hence also to new sections of text, even though he finally forbade his brothers to make any additions. The incidents mentioned above showed him too clearly that the pure gospel could be turned into something alien by a legalistic approach. All the same he was aware of yet another danger: the falsification of his gospel by 'glosses'.

The extent to which Francis differs from a legalistic misunderstanding is also shown by consideration of the content of the rule. Originally Francis simply took passages from the Bible without making any direct application of them. They speak with the same urgency and toughness as in the gospel—as a summons, the actual realisation of which remains left to the individual Franciscan. Other biblical passages are adapted to particular situations and treated flexibly. Thus Matt. 19:21 is quoted with its injunction to sell what you possess and give to the poor. What is important for Francis is the demonstrative break with the past, and thus a general pattern of behaviour is deduced from this. Nevertheless the text is not misunderstood in a legalistic fashion: 'If anyone who seeks admission to the Order cannot dispose of his property without hindrance, although he is spiritually minded to do so, he should leave it all behind him, and that is enough.'[31] Another example is the way that in sending out his disciples Jesus tells them not to take any sandals or shoes (Matt. 10:10). But Francis' interpretation runs: 'Those who are obliged by necessity can wear shoes.'[32]

These two examples bring out the permissive character of the Franciscan interpretation of the Bible. It is shown also by the way in which according to the rule Franciscans 'can' and 'may' do an enormous number of things, as I have pointed out in another study:[33] there is very little that is expressly forbidden them. To say this is not to dispute the radical approach to the Bible shown by Francis and his brothers. It is simply to say that they do not do this in a legalistic frame of mind but with a spiritual dynamism that encourages life and imagination and in a freedom in which new horizons are continually opening out.

This is expressed most emphatically in the letter to Brother Leo: 'In what ever way you think you will best please our Lord and follow in his footsteps and in poverty, take that way with the Lord God's blessing and my obedience.'[34]

5. REGRESSIVE OR PROGRESSIVE EXEGESIS

As a movement of reaction fundamentalism aims at restoration. Its purpose is to turn the wheel of history back and to rebuild on the 'fundamental truths'.

The Franciscan movement too appeals to the settled foundation that has to be observed as the constructive principle of Christian reform.[35] But when one looks more closely one cannot discern any tendencies towards restoration in this movement of reform. With its interpretation of the Bible, that is with its scale of values and its way of life, it is juridically and theologically something new. The biographies fall over themselves in stressing this novelty.[36] Canon law has no provision for this kind of way of life, and so it is only by means of dispensation (the 'privilege of absolute poverty') that the pope can guarantee it a place within the Church.[37] Theology for its part resists the pastoral practice of the mendicant orders with dogmatic arguments that a hundred years earlier had been put forward by the pope himself.[38]

The conclusion to be drawn from this is that Francis displayed an innovatory and progressive understanding of Scripture.

6. ABSOLUTE OR SACRAMENTAL EXEGESIS

Thanks to its theory of verbal inspiration, fundamentalism runs the danger of placing all biblical passages on the same level, isolating them from each other and absolutising them. What it at least tends to overlook is that these have their own internal context. They can only be interpreted if the principle of coherence is observed.

In Francis this takes the form of a sacramental perspective that even includes atheist or pagan or indeed ordinary everyday writings: 'Therefore, whenever he would find anything written, whether about God or about men, along the way, or in a house, or on the floor, he would pick it up with the greatest reverence and put it in a sacred or decent place, lest the name of the Lord or anything else pertaining to it might be written on it. One day when he was asked by a certain brother why he so diligently picked up writings even of pagans or writings in which there was no mention of the name of the Lord, he replied: "Son, because the letters are there out of which the most glorious name of the Lord God could be put together. Whatever is good there does not pertain to the pagans, nor to any other men, but to God alone, to whom belongs every good." And what is no less to be admired, when he had caused some letters of greeting or admonition to be written, he would not allow even a single letter or syllable to be deleted, even though they had often been placed there superfluously or in error.'[39] Every word and every sentence, however profane or banal its context, pointed to something. What was really meant, the profound meaning of every passage and every speech, is according to Francis the word of the living God, the word that through Mary 'took on our weak human nature',[40] before which one should 'fall to the ground and adore him with fear and reverence'.[41] In this attitude to the written word Francis differed from all the ideas of his contemporaries. Not only did he ascribe the word the same significance as the sacrament but even gave it precedence: 'We know his Body is not present unless the bread is first consecrated by these words.'[42]

The literal observance of the gospel by Francis of Assisi has thus to be understood on the basis of the focus that gives it meaning, Jesus Christ. As far as he is concerned there is no exegesis apart from this focus.

7. DOGMATIC OR COMMEMORATIVE EXEGESIS

Thanks to its theory of verbal inspiration fundamentalism also comes close to a purely dogmatic exegesis, an often anaemic doctrine (and that in certain circumstances on the part of the *magisterium*): hence its inherent intolerance.

For Francis it is self-evident that he should wish to live the true faith within and with the Church.[43] He is disturbed by the idea of the orthodoxy of his community being threatened.[44] Orthodoxy is indeed a condition for enrolment.[45]

At the same time it should be noted that orthodoxy always includes orthopraxis, which in the terminology of his age Francis calls 'a life of penance' and is equivalent to a way of life consistently and radically committed to the gospel.[46] What is interesting in this context is the way Francis characterises his own exegesis of his rule: 'For this is a reminder (*recordatio*), admonition, exhortation, and my testament which I, Brother Francis, worthless as I am, leave to you, my brothers, that we may observe in a more Catholic way the Rule we have promised to God.'[47]

What Francis wants is therefore a dynamic exegesis on the basis of recollection and encouragement, not a dogmatic exegesis content to repeat things sentence by sentence. His exegesis is a matter of the heart (re-*cor*-datio),[48] not of the reason, of human devotion, not of abstraction, of passionate language and of the kind of witness shown by his testament, not of anaemic formulas and theories. But this already brings in a further point.

8. SCIENTIFIC OR PRACTICAL EXEGESIS

Because of the way in which it arose, fundamentalism's attitude towards scientific theology is one of rejection, directed first against the liberal school of theology but then extended to become a matter of principle.

To some extent Francis shares this attitude. Clearly he experienced book-learning as such as a real temptation,[49] to which his reaction was to express his solidarity with the unlettered masses.[50] One should not strive after a scholarly career. The brothers 'should realise instead that the only thing they should desire is to have the spirit of God at work within them, while they pray to him unceasingly with a heart free from self-interest. They must be humble, too, and patient in persecution or illness, loving those who persecute us by blaming us or bringing charges against us.'[51] The whole stress is thus placed on the existential or living interpretation of holy Scripture. Prayer and self-sacrifice are also the necessary pre-conditions for scholarly activity.[52]

The conclusion to be drawn from this is that Francis does not actually reject scholarship as such but simply a certain manner of conducting it. This method can best be characterised by explaining the 'gloss' mentioned above that Francis rejected so passionately. In editions of the Bible the practice was to explain passages that were not easily understood either in the margin or between the lines, producing marginal or interlinear glosses. With time these glosses gained the upper hand and finally developed into independent biblical commentaries.[53] Clearly they developed their own dynamism. More and more they disguised the original meaning of holy Scripture and often totally supplanted it in favour of theoretical considerations. Francis is thus resisting a purely academic and intellectual exegesis which in its encounter with Scripture no longer sees itself called into question but prefers its own constructions and distinctions.

In a chapter on true simplicity it says among other things: 'This is that simplicity that, not considering *Grecian glories for the best*, chooses rather to act than to learn or to teach. This is that simplicity that, in all the divine laws, leaves wordy circumlocutions, ornaments, and embellishments, vain displays and curiosities, to those who are marked for a fall, and seeks not the bark but the pith, not the shell but the kernel, not the many things, but the much, the greatest and the lasting good. The most holy father demanded this virtue in both the learned and the lay brothers, not considering it contrary to wisdom, but true wisdom's sister, though he thought it easier to be gotten as a habit and more ready to be used by those who are poor as regards learning.'[54] This for Francis is what is meant by the uncomplicated and unfeigned immediacy of the gospel and by the gospel itself that demands to be interpreted in practice and consistently in one's life.

The hostility to learning and scholarship is not as fundamental as has continually been asserted up to today. Francis himself demands the assistance of brothers learned in the Bible and skilled in the use of language, and, within the conditions of an existential and spiritual frame of reference, opens the way for theology. This, however, must not free itself from this frame of reference and build up a world of its own. For ultimately the gospel is only interpreted in Christian living. Scholarship and learning mediate between these as their servant.

Since it is only he or she who does the gospel that understands it, the first book of the gospels the young community possessed was given to a poor woman, 'since we are admonished by it to help the poor. I believe indeed that the gift of it will be more pleasing to God than our reading from it.'[55] To put it another way, Franciscan exegesis takes the risk of venturing into the realm of practical living before everything has been thought out and made safe. It makes the experiment of living with and from the gospel and experiences its spiritual character in action.

9. MYSTICISM

If one reads St Francis' writings, then in every line one notices the holy fire that burns in him. Everything is living experience, fulfilled being, 'spirit and life'. The various aspects set out above involved in the literal observance of the gospel already allow us dimly to discern the depths and the horizons these presuppose as far as his inner experience is concerned. Jesus, the gospel and God are for Francis a living reality that surprises and arouses him. The words alone are capable of putting him into a dynamic mystical state in which his heart is on fire and his language attains its greatest formal perfection. The canticle of the sun is simply the best-known poetic expression of his mystical experiences.

This mysticism differs essentially from other mystical tendencies which, if one reads the written evidence about them, occur without the gospel and Christ. For Francis the gospel is the medium by which his experience is continually nourished and Jesus Christ the lasting way to God. Hence they are central in word and sacrament.

This spiritual bond with the gospel shows the promises that lie in the actual form of Francis of Assisi.

10. OPPORTUNITIES FOR TODAY

In the literal observance of the gospel there is thus to be found an opportunity for today, especially if one avoids the misunderstandings of fundamentalism.

Following the Franciscan line, the Church, its exegesis, its theology, and its way of life must commit themselves to a personal, permissive, progressive, sacramental, commemorative and practical evangelicity. Then 'spirit and life' will be experienced. If on the other hand what prevails is fundamentalism with its objectified, prohibitive, regressive, absolute, dogmatic interpretation of the Bible, or a purely scientific and scholarly theology, then this would mean the death of the gospel and of the Church (or rather of those who encounter the gospel in this way). This would particularly apply if this fundamentalist understanding of the Bible were encouraged and promoted by a Church leadership aiming at restoration.

Translated by Robert Nowell

Notes

1. I. Schlauri *Saint François et la Bible: Essai bibliographique de sa Spiritualité évangélique, Collectanea Franciscana 40* (Rome 1970) pp. 365-437.

2. *Lettura biblico-teologica delle fonti francescane* ed. G. Gordaropoli and M. Conti (Rome 1979) including particularly: M. Conti *La sacra scrittura nell' esperienza e negli scritti di san Francesco: Criteri ermeneutici* pp. 19-59; L. Iriarte *Figure bibliche 'privilegiate' nell' itinerario spirituale di san Francesco* pp. 61-81; O. van Asseldonk *Insegnamenti biblici 'privilegiati' negli scritti di san Francesco d'Assisi* pp. 83-116; A. Sousa Costa *La dottrina ecclesiale della vita religiosa e il suo influsso sulla 'Forma vitae' di san Francesco* pp. 117-164; A. G. Matanic *'Novitas Franciscana': Francesco d'Assisi nel suo rapporto con le preesistenti forme e dottrine di vita religiosa* pp. 165-182. See also W. Egger *Nachfolge als Weg zum Leben. Chancen neuerer exegetischer Methoden dargelegt an Mk 10:17-31* (Klosterneuburg 1979) especially chapter 3, 'Ein Beispiel aus der Wirkungsgeschichte des Textes (Mk. 10:17-31) als der Text für Franz von Assisi' pp. 237-284; T. Matura *Die Lebensordnung nach dem Evangelium. Franziskus von Assisi damals und heute,* (Werl 1979); T. Matura *Le Projet évangélique de François d'Assise aujourd'hui,* (Paris 1977).

3. *Die Schriften des heiligen Franziskus von Assisi* ed. L. Hardick and E. Grau (Werl 1980); *Die Opuscula des heiligen Franziskus von Assisi. Neue textkritische Edition* ed. K. Esser (Grottaferrata/Rome 1976). English translations are cited from *St Francis of Assisi: Writings and Biographies. English Omnibus of the Sources for the Life of St Francis* ed. Marion A. Habig (Chicago 1973).

4. Conti, cited in note 2, pp. 20-24.

5. Iriarte, cited in note 2.

6. Asseldonk, cited in note 2.

7. Egger, cited in note 2, p. 268.

8. Conti, cited in note 2, pp. 27-45.

9. Asseldonk, cited in note 2; Matura, cited in note 2, p. 60.

10. Egger, cited in note 2, pp. 239-284; Matura, cited in note 2, p. 58.

11. Egger, cited in note 2, pp. 282-283.

12. Asseldonk, cited in note 2, p. 88; Egger, cited in note 2, p. 276. Both are using an expression of F. Mann's.

13. *Admonition* § 7, Habig p. 81.

14. Asseldonk, cited in note 2, p. 88.

15. Egger, cited in note 2, p. 279.

16. *Testament* § 38, Habig p. 69.

17. *'Compilatio Assisiensis' dagli Scritti di fr. Leone e Compagni su S. Francesco d'Assisi* ed. M. Bigaroni (Porziuncula 1975) § 17, Habig p. 1088.

18. Bigaroni § 102, Habig p. 1199.

19. Bigaroni § 52, Habig p. 1144.

20. J. P. Michael, s.v. 'Fundamentalismus' in *Lexikon für Theologie und Kirche*, IV (Freiburg-im-Breisgau 1960) cols. 451-452.

21. P. Walter 'Objektive und personale Wahrheit' in *Kirchenblatt für die reformierte Schweiz* 136 (Basle 1980) 50-51.

22. Thomas von Celano *Leben und Wunder des heiligen Franziskus von Assisi* (Werl ²1964) first life § 22 = 1 Cel. 22, pp. 246-247 Habig.

23. *Die Dreigefährtenlegende des heiligen Franziskus* (Werl 1972) §§ 28-29 = 3 Comp. §§ 28-29, Habig p. 917.

24. *Testament* § 14, Habig p. 68.

25. *Regula non bullata* (RNB) § 2:1, Habig p. 32; *Regula bullata* (RB) § 12:1, Habig p. 64.

26. *Admonition* 7:2-3, Habig p. 81.

27. *Sic et sic ordinate vivere.*

28. Bigaroni § 18, Habig pp. 1088-1089.

29. *Die Chronik des Bruders Jordan von Giano: Nach Deutschland und England* ed L. Hardick (Werl 1957) p. 12.

30. RNB § 1:13, Habig p. 34.

31. RNB § 2:11, Habig p. 32.

32. RNB §§ 14:2, 2:15; not in Habig.

33. A. Rotzetter 'Der franziskanische Mensch zwischen Autorität und Freiheit. Eine Re-Lectio der Regula non bullata des heiligen Franziskus' *Franziskanische Studien* 59 (Werl 1977) 97-124.

34. Letter to Leo §§ 3-4, Habig pp. 118-119.

35. 1 Cel. 18, Habig p. 244.

36. A. Rotzetter *Die Funktion der franziskanischen Bewegung in der Kirche. Eine pastoraltheologische Interpretation der grundlegenden franziskanischen Texte* (Schwyz 1977) pp. 191, 278-281; Matanic, cited in note 2.

37. Matanic, cited in note 2; A. Rotzetter 'Zuversicht aus dem Glauben: Franz von Assisi, in *Lebendige Seelsorge* 31 (1980) 211-212.

38. J. Ratzinger 'Der Einfluss des Bettelordensstreites auf die Entwicklung der Lehre vom päpstlichen Universalprimat. Unter besonderer Berücksichtigung des heiligen Bonaventura *Theologie in Geschichte und Gegenwart* (Munich 1957) 697-724.

39. 1 Cel. 82, Habig pp. 297-298.

40. Letter to the faithful II:4, Habig p. 93.

41. Letter to the order § 4, Habig pp. 103-104.

42. Letter to clerics § 2, Habig p. 101.

43. RNB § 23:7, Habig p. 51.

44. For example, *Testament* § 31, Habig p. 69.

45. RB § 2:2, Habig p. 58.

46. RNB § 23:7, *Testament* § 1, Habig pp. 51, 67.

47. *Testament* § 34, Habig p. 69.

48. Cf. 2 Cel. 102, Bigaroni § 79; Habig p. 446.

49. Bigaroni § 104, Habig pp. 1197-1198.

50. O. Schmucki 'Ignorans sum et idiota. Das Ausmass der schulischen Bildung des heiligen Franziskus von Assisi' *Studia historico-ecclesiastica. Festschrift für L. G. Spätling OFM* (Rome 1977) 283-310; *Testament* § 19, Habig p. 68.

51. RB § 10:7-8, Habig pp. 63-64.

52. Letter to Anthony, Habig p. 164.

53. J. Schmid and A. M. Stickler s.v. 'Glossen' in *Lexikon für Theologie und Kirche*, IV (Freiburg-im-Breisgau 1960) cols. 968-971.

54. 2 Cel. 159, Habig p. 513.

55. Bigaroni § 93; quotation in text from 2 Cel. 91, Habig p. 437.

Knut Walf

'My' Francis of Assisi?

'IF HEALTHY man is a social phenomenon, so is the sick man'. This quotation is from Robert Musil's novel *Der Mahn ohne Eigenschaften*[1] and it is taken from a passage in this unfinished monumental work in which Clarissa, Musil's novel figure, expresses the following thought about Francis of Assisi: '"The most important aspect", she wrote, "is that at that time a man, whom we would now undoubtedly put in a sanatorium and do so with good conscience, could live, teach and lead his contemporaries".'[2]

This quotation points to two realities. The first is that we are always coming across Francis of Assisi in contemporary literature and quite often in hidden places. The second is that it is difficult to understand him—his real place is in a sanatorium. In any case, Musil's Clarissa says elsewhere in the novel, what could have happened to Francis of Assisi at that time in a centre of culture is now possible only in a mountain village. Musil's—or Clarissa's—conclusion is this 'points to the dispossession of the religious experience'.[3]

It is not possible to provide a complete answer, within the space of this short article, to the question as to whether modern writers have been successful in their attempts to contribute to an understanding of Francis of Assisi or whether they have inevitably, on the basis of Musil's pessimistic evaluation, been doomed to failure. My answer must be incomplete, if only because a complete answer presupposes a critical reading of the very extensive biographical literature about Francis and that would be impossible for a single individual to carry out. He would have to read and assess some four hundred books already in existence—a number that is likely to be considerably increased in this 'year of Saint Francis'.

I have therefore limited my reading to a very small number of modern books on Francis which have had an influence in the German-speaking countries on the image of Francis: Adolf Holl's *Der letzte Christ—Franz von Assisi, Mein Franz von Assisi*, a work by the Greek author, Nikos Kazantzakis, who died in Germany in 1957, and *Bruder Feuer*, by Luise Rinser, who has lived in Italy for many years. All three writers have tried to make the figure and the life of Francis of Assisi accessible to modern readers. In this task, Holl has kept most closely to the attested historical facts, while Rinser has avoided making the leap across the intervening centuries and has instead transposed the figure of Francis into the social context of modern Italy.

1. THE MOTIVATION

The first question that comes to mind is why these three authors were so drawn to the figure of Francis that they tried, with the literary means at their disposal, to refashion this historical figure and present him in a very comprehensive way. Holl, an Austrian priest teaching comparative religion at the University of Vienna, came into conflict with the Church in 1973 because of other publications and was forbidden to teach. He was suspended in 1976. At the very beginning of his book on Francis, he provides a 'declaration of intention', in which he says that he 'does not wish to give abstract knowledge, but wants contemporary social structures to be better understood and not seen as the result of pure chance' (H., p. 29f).[4] Kazantzakis says in the Preface to his book that he has left out, changed and added a great deal in order to 'bring the saint's life closer to his myth'. Rinser sees clear parallels between our own times and those of Francis, with the result that Francis can 'give us answers to many questions' (R., p. 11). She describes her attempt to transpose Francis' life and work to our own period in a very striking way as a 'writing of a pop history of Francis of Assisi' (R., p. 13).

2. THE FRANCIS OF THE AUTHORS

Whereas, in Rinser's presentation, Francis does not appear himself, he dominates in Holl's like a leading actor on the stage. Does Holl see Francis as acting the principle of poverty? He claims, certainly, that 'he (= Francis) needs spectators' (H., p. 70). The Francis drawn by Rinser as a character in a pious strip cartoon is not unlike Holl's actor and behaves like a Superman who solves all problems with an incredible use of understatement. For Kazantzakis, 'Saint Francis is the model of the fighter' (Preface).

The descriptions of Francis' conversion that these three authors give are also widely divergent. Was that conversion the result of a sudden experience or was it perhaps caused by family influences or even by heredity? Holl refers to Mockler's hypothesis, according to which 'Francis' father was a secret heretic, possibly even a Catharist' (H., p. 72). Kazantzakis, on the other hand, stresses the hereditary influence of Francis' French mother, 'who had the blood of troubadours and other crack-brained men in her veins' (K., p. 58). From the very beginning, Francis' biographers, such as Thomas Celano, saw a parallel between his conversion and that of Augustine, with the result that Francis was described as a dissolute and depraved young man before he was converted. Despite the ease with which this picture of the young Francis can be proved wrong by critical historical research, Rinser still prefers to present Francis, once again, as a 'wild playboy' and a 'lover of girls and parties' (R., p. 9), who radically changed his way of life 'from one day to the next' (R., p. 67).

Each author also provides a very different account of Francis' motives and aims. Holl certainly does not present him as a saint, although he does not doubt for a moment that he was a saint. He has his readers' interest so much at heart, however, that he says openly that 'the majority of people in an industrial society . . .' would have 'only very vague and insipid feelings' if Francis were described as a saint (H., p. 13). What, then, is Francis? Is he perhaps a kind of saint of the class war? Holl stresses that he 'disclaimed his membership of the most powerful class of the period' and fought 'for every proposition in his programme'—to such an extent that Holl is unable to describe him as politically moderate.

Rinser sees Francis as the founder and leader of a commune, the structure and aims of which are reminiscent of the movement of Longo Mai. He is, for her, a voluntary worker, not in the Third World, but in his own country, Italy. His people 'built dams and reservoirs and terraces' (R., p. 35). Later, however, she corrects herself, saying that what he wanted was not a commune, but a community. Rinser's Franciscan community, however, often displays all the characteristics of a modern youth sect of the kind that fifteen-year-old schoolchildren join when they cannot bear to stay at home any longer (R., p. 94f). She also mentions Zen Buddhism (or Master Eckhart), although perhaps not explicitly. Francis says this, for example, about a young person who is looking for God: 'He is looking here, there and everywhere for God and cannot find him. He might have been able to find him here, while he was cleaning' (R., p. 96f).

It is therefore reasonable to ask in what religious or spiritual context these three authors place Francis. They clearly prefer to give him a place in their own world-view rather than engage in a tedious search for the man himself. It is not in any sense the historical Francis of Assisi who interests any of these contemporary writers, but, as Kazantzakis openly proclaims in the very title of his book, it is a question of 'my' Francis.

Holl's aim is to use his interpretation of Francis to reach a better understanding of contemporary relationships in society, but he looks for an explanation of the man far back in history, not in Francis' own times, but between then and now, in the figure of Luther. What Francis and Luther have in common, Holl believes, is that neither could find any effective help in the conventional religion of their own period (H., p. 175). Holl also compares Francis with Buddha and says that, when we recall the legend of the wolf of Gubbio, Francis stands 'before us as a veritable Buddha' (H., p. 184). It is also not difficult for this author to imagine that Francis would have 'become a mystic if he had lived at that time among Muslims or in India' (H., p. 285).

Max Picard has made us familiar with the idea that 'Hitler lives in us' and Holl similarly reaches the conclusion at the end of his speculations about Francis that he also lives in all of us 'as one of those suppressed longings of our middle-class constitution' (H., p. 334). We middle-class citizens constantly experience a downward pull. 'Down there' points to a way of life that is not yet marked with the harsh need to reject all impulses (H., p. 359). Do we, then, find Francis likeable because he lived consistently in the way that we, as middle-class people, would secretly like to live? Is he the symbol of all those unexpressed middle-class desires and imaginings?

Rinser's Francis also has signs of that exotic element that seems so to fascinate young contemporary members of the middle class. She believes that his Canticle of the Sun 'was really Indian; the Hindus also have the feeling that nothing matters very much' (R., p. 70). She has this to say about his community: 'In our society too, there are people who are not Christians; we have several Hindus and a Mohammedan and a number of atheists, if that is what we can call them' (R., p. 85). Is this seeing Francis as a precursor of an all too accommodating syncretism?

3. THE FASCINATION OF FRANCIS OF ASSISI

I have already pointed out that all three authors have fashioned a Francis of their own. We must, however, look more closely at their books if we are to detect which aspects and peculiarities of the man fascinate the authors. It must, however, be stated in advance that it would be impossible to form even a relatively consistent picture of Francis, however attentively one followed the representations of the different authors. The range stretches from Francis as a second Christ to Francis the turncoat and from an inspired simpleton who was weary of life to a masochist.

Kazantzakis' hero is sketched out with particular clarity as a second Jesus and it is inevitable that, in so doing, the author often borders on sentimentality and nonsense. Some of his statements are reminiscent of and even echo the gospels, but he frequently inserts new signs and symbols into these passages. For example, in one case he says: 'Francis took a handful of ash from the hearth and threw it into the soup. The brethren at once recognised him' (K., p. 176). Similar passages can also be found in Rinser's *Bruder Feuer*. Modern versions of pericopes from the gospels concern her more than the legends of Francis himself. He enters a forbidden military zone at night-time, for example, and persuades a professional soldier who is on guard duty there to follow him: 'I command you in the name of him in whom you have been baptised to lay down your arms. God is a God of the living and the loving! Come!' (R., p. 89).

Is it surprising, then, that people call this remarkable saint the 'turncoat'? Or is he just an inspired simpleton who is weary of life? Are such strange and peculiar characteristics not necessarily the results of an attempt to transpose the figure of an extraordinary medieval man into the present? Dramatic events which must have made a deep impression on medieval people have the effect today of rather faded cabaret acts. An example of this is the scene in which Francis undresses in front of the crowd and the bishop, who was inclined towards the left and therefore called by Rinser the 'Red Bishop', 'until he was stark naked' (R., p. 107). We can only wait at this point, with Robert Musil, until the police appear on the scene and take this Francis as quickly as possible to a sanatorium. But (of course) nothing of the kind happens in Rinser's account. She makes her 'Red Bishop' throw a coat around Francis. And it is the bishop and not Francis who has to bear the further consequences of these incredible events. The bishop has been worn down in the course of time by 'people' and then 'he was summoned to Rome, to the Vatican, where he was cold-shouldered. Yes, that is how it was' (R., p. 107). We might add here: Yes, it is as easy as that to explain Francis to modern readers. Or perhaps it isn't?

Holl has succeeded better than the other two authors in explaining the figure of Francis of Assisi to modern readers, I think, but even he cannot prevent critics from misunderstanding what Reinhold Schneider has called an 'extreme existence'. Manfred Müller, for example, ended his detailed discussion of Holl's book in the German news magazine *Der Spiegel* with these words: 'I find it difficult to discover a Christian at all in such a fakir'.

It is certainly easy to react in this way after reading all these books about Francis. I myself have great difficulty in discovering a Christian in Kazantzakis' Francis and I certainly cannot discover a historically attested Francis. I am inclined to think that Kazantzakis is presenting us with a sectarian or an evil Manichaean who despises everything to do with the body. What does the saint's steep path to holiness look like? 'You reach God as a rag, a handful of hair and bones, smelling of filth and incense' (K., p. 98). He has himself whipped by his constant companion Leo until the blood pours from him and he goes on screaming: 'Harder! Harder! You are pitying the whore Flesh!' (K., p. 238).

This, of course, brings us back to the Francis who has been called a masochist. There is no doubt that episodes concerning Francis which border on that aberration have been handed down. Holl reports that Francis, although he was only half healed, removed his cowl in the depths of winter, put a halter round his neck and let one of his brethren lead him by it in front of the assembled people. He did this as a penance for having eaten meat and drunk meat-broth while he was still sick (H., p. 317).

Kazantzakis' Francis is presented throughout as a very strange figure with masochistic tendencies. He has himself beaten whenever the opportunity arises and praises God as the blows fall. As the author says: 'The flesh may one day become spirit' (K., p. 73). He calls out to stone-throwing children: 'If you throw a stone at me, God will bless you once. If you throw two stones, he will bless you twice. If you throw three, he will bless you three times' (K., p. 66). On one occasion, women and children in a 'wild' village stone him almost to death, but he calls out to them: 'Thank you, my children! Hail to you!' (K., p. 131).

Because the author often presents us with scenes like this without connecting them with any ascetic purpose, we are bound to have the impression that this Francis is a wrong-headed masochist. He reacts with panic to any sexual stimulus: 'He tore the rope from his waist and I heard him beating his back and thighs like a madman all through the night. Early next morning, he jumped up stark naked. His body was blue and swollen with the cold and from his wounds' (K., p. 201).

Rinser's Francis also enjoys suffering, although he does it in solidarity with the hungry and those in prison (R., p. 104ff). In this, Rinser comes closest of all three authors to the attitude that the historical Francis had towards voluntarily undertaken suffering and deprivation. Nonetheless, we still feel constrained to question some of her attempts to portray Francis in modern literary terms. Examples of this are Rinser's incredible account of Francis' imprisonment, tied night and day to an iron ring on the wall of the cellar in his father's house, and his renunciation of the woman who worships him, Paola—a declaration which sounds so patently insincere: 'If you were living as you ought to live . . . you would be closer to me than if you were lying in my arms! Don't cry! Be happy!' (R., p. 112). It should not be forgotten that it is a twentieth century Francis who is speaking these words!

This brings us to another peculiar aspect, not only of Rinser's Francis, but also of the man as presented by the other two authors. All three of them show him as strangely hostile to women. Holl refers to the historical sources, according to which Francis was exposed to severe 'temptations of the flesh'. One of the titbits that Holl offers his readers comes straight from Thomas Celano, but is adapted by the author. To resist one of these temptations, Francis went one frosty winter's night into the garden and made seven heaps of snow. Then he said to himself: 'Look, this big heap of snow is your wife!' (H., p. 161). Holl tries very hard to make the modern reader understand these extremely ascetic aspects of his Francis especially by his sympathetic portrayal of Francis' relationship with Clare.

Kazantzakis, on the other hand, describes Francis' strange attitude to women in very harsh language. This applies in particular to his description of Francis' meeting with Clare. Francis rejects Clare's suggestion that she will lead a life similar to his quite fiercely: 'I don't trust women! Eve's serpent has been licking your lips and ears for thousands of years! Do not lead me into temptation! . . . Get up and go back home! We don't want women!' (K., p. 208). This scene is followed by an event that gives a very archaic impression. Francis behaves like a witch-doctor in it: 'Francis growled, roared, bleated like a lamb and howled like a wolf'. Yet the scene ends with an incredible transformation of Francis himself and an invitation to Clare to join his community.

Later, however, Kazantzakis' Francis once again becomes a fierce misogynist who regards God as the only one who can really tame women: 'He alone can tame that wild beast woman! Only he can do it!' (K., p. 222). It is therefore only reasonable to expect this Francis to refuse to visit Clare and her companions in their convent. Kazantzakis also makes use here of the symbol that he has so often employed elsewhere in his writing—that of the combination of rain and earth: 'Rain is clean and earth is clean. But when they come together they become dirt. This is what happens to the hands of a man and a woman when they joint together' (K., p. 225).

Like her Francis, Rinser's Clare also comes from a rich family. She is also very beautiful and 'had ten admirers hanging from each of her fingers' (R., p. 33). Francis and Clare love one another, but 'their love story had never been an ordinary one. Francis had many girl-friends, but Clare had from the very beginning always been quite different for him' (R., p. 33). Because people are talking about them, Francis suggests 'at the end of December' that they should not meet again until the roses bloom. And, as in the traditional legend, the miracle of the wild roses takes place in the twentieth century—'they bloomed as though it were June' (R., p. 115).

The authors, then, are clearly fascinated by Francis' attitude towards women. In the same way, they are very interested in his scepticism towards the study of theology. Holl in particular presents him 'chatting with all the Christian theologians in heaven— Aurelius Augustine, Karl Barth, Thomas Aquinas and Rudolf Bultmann. He asks them what they would have been without their books. They have no suitable answer to give him. He then says: "Without your books, you might have become Christians"' (H., p. 104).

There is a striking parallel in Kazantzakis' story of Francis between the first appearance of the man as a witch-doctor who is hostile to women, which I have already mentioned, and a second scene concerned with books and Francis' hatred of them. Kazantzakis situates this second episode in the period after Francis' return from Palestine. During his absence, his community has changed fundamentally. Many of his brethren have become fascinated by theology in nearby Bologna. Kazantzakis makes Francis call out: 'These educated men are wolves that have broken into our sheepfold. I want nothing to do with the wise sayings of the brain—Satan is in them. God is in the heart. The heart does not want learning and has never consulted a book. Where are we going? Down into the abyss!' (K., p. 210ff). This is followed by the scene that, in Kazantzakis' account, immediately follows the scene with Clare. This time, Francis goes for the young brother who is thirsty for knowledge and who had managed to obtain a book that attempted to interpret the resurrection of Christ theologically. Francis tears it out of his hands with the words: '"I won't let you keep it!" he cried out in anger and threw the book into the fire. "Ashes! Ashes!" he cried and, a little later: "Cursed is the spirit of man!"' (K., p. 211).

4. THE GOD OF FRANCIS OF ASSISI

In the previous section, I have given two examples of Kazantzakis' presentation of Francis with clear characteristics of a witch-doctor or perhaps more accurately of a shaman. The critic of Holl's book whom I have already mentioned was not able to discover a Christian in Francis as depicted by the author of *Francis—the Last Christian*. We are therefore bound to ask: What is the God of the Francis of these three authors?

The God of Kazantzakis' Francis is an archaic God with whom man can come into contact through images of the elements. God is 'like a glass of fresh water'. He is also like fire: 'God is a funeral pyre. . . . He burns and we burn to death on him' (K., p. 19). There is no road leading to this God. There is only the abyss and whoever wants to find him must leap in. Kazantzakis' God is therefore also a God of the earth as well as a God of water and fire and he lives in the pit of that earth.

The end of all those who are seeking God is lamentation, whether they have found him or not. Why? Brother Leo, Francis' companion, provides the answer: 'I don't know. They all cry' (K., p. 28). But God is also to be found everywhere in nature. Francis calls to him: 'I know you are everywhere. I find you when I lift a stone. I look into your face when I plunge into a fountain. When I look at a caterpillar, I see your name engraved on its back' (K., p. 62). The same God, however, also demands that he should let himself be stoned by children. He is far beyond man's capacity to understand. He is immeasurable: 'Man lives within the measure. God lives beyond the measure' (K., p. 71).

In Rinser's book, Francis seeks God in ordinary things and everyday activities. He explicitly rejects all special means of seeking God (R., p. 96)—I have already indicated this above. Rinser's Francis is less of a seeker after God than a contemporary who tries to imitate Jesus consistently. She therefore has less to say about God and all the more to say about how Jesus' message can be made present here and now.

Holl's presentation points in the same direction, although he does not change the historical perspective. He insists again and again that he does not want to present Francis as a saint out of consideration, as we have already seen above, for 'the majority of people in an industrial society' who would have 'only very vague and insipid feelings' if he were to portray the man as a saint (H., p. 13). There are, however, considerable differences between Rinser's and Holl's images of Jesus.

In Rinser's presentation, Francis is so inspired by the life and the figure of the historical Jesus that it has the effect of making him a social revolutionary. At the same time, however, this has an indirect retrospective effect on her image of Jesus, with the result that it is, in this book at least, very vague indeed. Holl, on the other hand, stresses that Francis' Jesus is a Jesus who has been 'mediated by the Church' (H., p. 88). He is certainly not that in Rinser's portrayal. It is precisely the official representatives of the Church who find it difficult even to begin to understand Rinser's Francis. Apart from the 'Red Bishop' whom I have mentioned above, they are the representatives of law and order and they defend the established structures of society. As the parish priest of Sant'Anna says: 'Francis does not work in our sense of the word. His plans are not ours' (R., p. 54).

It emerges very clearly from these books how difficult it is—indeed, it is almost impossible—to grasp the social aims of the historical Francis with the help of our contemporary categories of thought. Holl says that 'Francis' teaching that we should possess nothing' is 'social and political dynamite' (H., p. 113). There are enough examples of this in his own life and in the history of the early Franciscan movement, but this dynamite acts in little streams and narrow, almost invisible channels. It is therefore hardly surprising that these authors have the greatest difficulty in discovering a really political dimension in Francis' programme. Was he ultimately only concerned with the individual and his salvation? Where is the social dimension?

5. THE AUTHORS' MODELS

It is clear from a comparison of these three contemporary authors' portraits of Francis that they have become frozen models under the pressure of the authors' own ideas and expectations. Even Holl's representation, which is the closest to the known historical facts, has been forced into the Procrustes' bed of his own presuppositions. How otherwise could he claim that Francis was the 'last Christian' (the title of his book) 'before the vehicle of progress finally roared off for ever' (H., p. 10). It would seem that a certain desire for flight on the part of the authors lurks behind their interpretation of Francis. In the case of Holl, it is obviously a longing to retreat from the threshold of the age of the bourgeoisie. It is similar in the case of Rinser, who is, however, able to conceal this desire to run away by using the literary device of transposing Francis into the twentieth century. Kazantzakis, who is the furthest removed of the three authors from the historical Francis, conjures up an archaic world in which Francis moves about like a witch-doctor and can hardly be understood by us. This author is, however, honest and calls his book '*My* Francis of Assisi'. The proportions would have been retained if both Holl and Rinser had entitled their books '*My* Francis'.

It is, however, also obvious that the legends about the fascinating figure of Francis of Assisi, which began to flourish even while he was still alive, are still being formed today. If we look at it in this way, then these three authors have woven a little more of the centuries-old fabric of Francis-legends. His message and indeed simply his life have always provided many points of contact to which ideas for reforming the Church and society could be legitimately connected. And this is still clearly the case. Both individuals and groups claimed him when he was alive and active and they still continue to claim him today—and these individuals and groups have always been extremely diverse. Will a closer and more critical look at the situation, however, perhaps not reveal that the very wide spectrum of this appeal to Francis may in itself be simply a series of vain attempts to justify him or those making the appeal? Did Francis himself not find it necessary to defend himself against a use of his message that he did not want?

He cannot now defend himself against those who attempt to interpret him, but it is still possible to be sceptical in one's attitude towards what contemporary interpreters of Francis make of him and to be critical in his place. 'My' Francis is, after all, not the Francis of the authors, but that is precisely what I have in common with them.

Translated by David Smith

Notes

1. Robert Musil *Der Mann ohne Eigenschaften. Gesammelte Werks* 5 (Reinbek 1978), p. 1734.
2. *Ibid.* p. 1801.
3. *Op. cit.*
4. Adolf Holl *Der letzte Christ—Franz von Assisi* (Stuttgart 1979); Nikos Kazantzakis *Mein Franz von Assisi* (Munich and Berlin 1979); Luise Rinser *Bruder Feuer* (Frankfurt 1978). Quotations from these books are indicated in the text in the following way: Holl = H.; Kazantzakis = K.; Rinser = R.; followed by the page number.

Eric Doyle

Select Bibliography on the Life and Message of St Francis

ST FRANCIS was born eight hundred years ago. No-one then had the faintest notion that in the person and life of this man, humanity would reach one of its finest and most authentic expressions. It is hardly surprising, therefore, that we should want to remember him. As our memory travels back over the eight centuries, it finds it cannot stop at St Francis. It is compelled to keep going until it comes to the one who made St Francis possible, Jesus Christ the Lord. St Francis is a model of Christian discipleship and his life was a kind of exegesis of the gospel, an exegesis that has never gone out of date. It is as fresh and attractive now as it was when he was alive.

The memory of St Francis stirs the heart. It tells us that individual efforts to make brotherhood and peace realities in our world are not futile, never lost. Individuals can change the course of history and renew the face of the earth. Our memory of St Francis engenders hope for the future. St Francis presents us now with a challenge to face the responsibilities we have to the centuries that are yet to come. The holiness of St Francis was a gift to humanity. His life remains a mystery of God's enlightening and strengthening grace.

If we desire to enter this mystery we can do nothing better than begin with the Saint's own writings which put us in close contact with his experience of God in Jesus Christ. The best text is the critical edition by K. Esser, OFM, *Opuscula Sancti Patris Assisiensis* (Grottaferrata, Rome 1978). It is available now in an excellent German edition with introduction and commentaries by Lothar Hardick, OFM, and Engelbert Grau, OFM, *Die Schriften des heiligen Franziskus von Assisi* (Werl/Westf., 1980). Editions based on Esser's critical text will be appearing shortly in other languages.

There is a rich collection of sources on St Francis himself and the early history of the Order. A good, brief and concise introduction is *Approccio Storico-Critico alle Fonti Francescane* (ed. Antonianum, Rome 1979). This will introduce the student to the fascinating and intricate questions about the relationship of the sources to one another, their provenance and authorship.

Among the early sources the writings of Thomas of Celano are indispensable. He entered the Order in 1215 and he knew St Francis personally. He wrote *The First Life of St Francis* within some three years of the Saint's death. *The Second Life of St Francis* was composed in the late 1240s for which he used additional material sent to the Minister General, Crescentius of Jesi, by close companions of St Francis. A fine edition of these materials, drawn up by the early companions in 1246, has been published in a parallel Latin-English version by R. B. Brooke, *The Writings of Leo, Rufino and Angelo, Companions of St Francis* (Oxford 1970). It gives first-hand knowledge by those who were with St Francis.

The Major Life of St Francis, composed by St Bonaventure between 1260 and 1263, is a spiritual biography by his most illustrious follower. It has received harsh treatment from a number of modern historians, for instance, P. Sabatier, A. G. Little, J. Moorman and R. B. Brooke, as having had a 'political' motive, namely to reconcile the differing factions in the Order at that time. This is an unjust assessment. St Bonaventure's work cannot be judged satisfactorily in exclusively historical terms. It is the work of a learned and creative theologian which presents St Francis as a model of gospel perfection and an exemplar of the evangelical virtues of poverty, humility, obedience, meekness and purity of heart. Indeed, St Francis is presented as an eschatological figure sent to the world in this final age, to renew the gospel life and to inflame people's hearts with the love of God. For St Bonaventure the crucial fact about St Francis was his mission, the new charism given to the Church by the Holy Spirit.

There are three other texts the popularity of which never seems to wane. They have been translated into many modern languages and published in various editions. The *Sacrum Commercium*, or as one English translation has it: *The Sacred Romance of St Francis with Lady Poverty*, was written between 1227 and 1245, probably nearer the earlier date. It is an enchanting allegory which describes how St Francis and a group of his friars sought out the Lady Poverty who had withdrawn to a high mountain. She instructs St Francis and his companions, and the piece ends with a banquet at which they all share a meal of crusts of bread and cold water. The text tells us that Lady Poverty asked to be shown the cloister. They took her to a hill and, pointing to the whole world before her, said: 'This, Lady, is our cloister.' The word *commercium* in the Latin title of the allegory would be better translated 'pact' or even better still 'covenant', for St Francis and his companions resolved to live the poverty of Christ, who is himself the New Covenant between God and humanity. *The Mirror of Perfection*, compiled from earlier sources in 1318, though somewhat polemical in character, gives an interesting picture of life at the Portiuncula, that blessed place where St Francis heard the gospel message that changed his life, where he spent so much of his time and where finally he met Sister Death in 1226. The third of these popular writings is the *Fioretti* or *The Little Flowers of St Francis*. It was written about 1330 and it presents a most faithful picture of the dynamic and attractive personality of St Francis.

Besides the writings of St Francis and the early written sources of his life and message, there remains still one more source: the city of Assisi itself. It is one of the holy places of the earth, of which Evelyn Underhill said: 'its soul is more manifest than any other city that I have ever known.' It is a source in two senses. First, the spirit of St Francis pervades its every inch. It is filled with an atmosphere of brotherhood, love and peace which no amount of commercialism ever manages to smother. Second, its medieval buildings, holy places and Giotto's frescoes reveal dimensions of St Francis' person and life that no written source can possibly hope to communicate. All this is to suggest, I suppose, that anyone who wants to penetrate the mystery of St Francis, really ought to visit Assisi. Where that is not possible, one can turn to the attractive publication *Assisi* (Narni-Terni, ed. Plurigraf, 1978), which takes one on an exciting pictorial tour of the city. Then there is R. Brown's *True Joy from Assisi. The Assisi Experience of Inner Peace and Joy* (Chicago 1978). It is a wonderful book which shows how Assisi can bring out the contemplative in all of us. The author has assembled a series of testimonies, from about fifty writers, to the spiritual effect Assisi had on them. No-one, I think, who reads this book will close it without a desire to go to Assisi.

Anyone who starts out on a study of St Francis and his evangelical movement, sooner or later comes across the name of P. Sabatier. It is no exaggeration to say that he initiated a new era in Franciscan studies. His brilliant, passionate and provocative *Vie de S. François d'Assise* which went into many editions and translations, remains a classical study of the life of St Francis. G. K. Chesterton's book *St Francis of Assisi*, reveals beyond doubt the heart of the Saint and what can only be called the utter genius of his holiness. Above all, Chesterton understood, as few have done, I think, St Francis' love of particulars, of individual people, of animals, birds and stones. He writes with discernment and wisdom: 'I have said that St Francis deliberately did not see the wood for the trees. It is even more true that St Francis deliberately did not see the mob for the men.' For a penetrating analysis of St Francis' spiritual journey and enlightening reflections on the virtues of poverty, humility and perfect joy, there is the admirable work by E. Longpré, OFM, *François d'Assise et son expérience spirituelle* (Paris 1966).

For those who would wish to pursue their interest in St Francis, a convenient and comprehensive research bibliography is provided in the second, revised and augmented English edition of O. Engelbert *St Francis of Assisi. A Bibliography* (Chicago 1965). The text of the life of St Francis is followed by eight *Appendices* concerning various aspects of the life and writings of St Francis, and extensive notes to the text. A comprehensive and detailed presentation of the topographical and social background is provided by A. Fortini *Nova Vita di San Francesco*, 4 Vols. (Assisi 1959).

On the writings of St Francis there are a number of very important scholarly works which are both instructive and edifying. D. Flood, OFM, published a careful and detailed study on the Rule of 1221, sometimes called 'The First Rule', which gives a critical edition and analysis of the text: *Die Regula non bullata der Minderbrüder* (Werl/Westf., 1967). This Rule was never approved for the Order. The English edition under the title *The Birth of a Movement: A Study of the First Rule of St Francis* (Chicago 1975), is made up of three parts. The first by D. Flood, treats of the historical context and formation of the Rule and gives an analysis of the text. We are given a graphic picture of the development of the early fraternity and understand clearly the use of the word 'movement' to describe the first decade of the Order's history. This is followed, in the second part, by an English translation of the Rule by P. Schwartz, OFM, and P. Lachance, OFM. The third part by T. Matura, OFM, examines the nature of the Franciscan charism and puts some searching questions to the Franciscan Order today. Matura's text was originally published in the French edition of the book: *La Naissance d'un Charisme* (Paris 1976).

The most scholarly modern works on the Rule of 1223, which the Order follows today, and the Testament of St Francis, which he wrote shortly before he died in 1226, were written by K. Esser, *Die Endgültige Regel der Minderen Brüder im Lichte der Neuesten Forschung* (Werl/Westf., 1965), and *Das Testament des Heiligen Franziskus von Assisi. Eine Untersuchung über seine Echtheit und seine Bedeutung* (Münster 1949). These works are indispensable for any critical study of the Rule and Testament of St Francis. Esser's study of the Rule is also an edifying presentation of the spirit of the Rule and its unique character. There is an English version of this, including a translation of spiritual conferences on the Testament by Esser, which had not previously been published in any language: *Rule and Testament of St Francis. Conferences to the Modern Followers of Francis* (Chicago 1977). A beautiful and deeply moving study of the Testament in the light of the biblical concept of the covenant, is the work by A. van Corstanje, OFM, *Het Verbond van Gods Armen* (Brummen 1962). An augmented and revised French version was then published: *Un Peuple de Pèlerins: Essai d'Interprétation biblique du Testament de Saint François* (Paris 1964), and subsequently an English version which added five chapters on the biblical background for covenant and poverty: *The Covenant with God's Poor. An Essay on the Biblical Interpretation of the Testament of St Francis of Assisi* (Chicago 1966). Van Corstanje's study is undoubtedly one of the finest theological reflections on Franciscanism published for many years.

The Canticle of Brother Sun is perhaps the most famous, but certainly the most beautiful, of the writings of St Francis. A remarkable study for depth of insight and originality, is the book by E. Leclerc, OFM, *Le Cantique des Créatures ou les Symboles de l'Union* (Paris 1970). Leclerc interprets *The Canticle of Brother Sun* as a symbolic expression of an experience that unfolds in the night of the soul. He demonstrates that the interior and exterior cannot be separated in any satisfactory interpretation of St Francis' mysticism. Leclerc discovered in the primary cosmic meaning of *The Canticle* another meaning that is of the interior order.

In November 1979 Pope John Paul II declared St Francis the Patron of the Environment. St Francis looked on the whole of creation as a vast fraternity with Brother Christ at its centre. He gave the name of sister or brother to every creature. It is instructive that one of the reasons why he composed *The Canticle of Brother Sun*, more than seven hundred years ago, was to protest at the misuse of creatures by human beings. How much more guilty we are today than they were in the middle ages. On the ecological significance of *The Canticle*, E. Doyle, OFM, has published a useful book: *St Francis and the Song of Brotherhood* (London 1980). The book was written for everyone who is concerned about the environment and the senseless destruction of so much precious life and matter. If water is our sister, as St Francis said, then how can we put her to death as we do, by pouring toxic acids into our lakes and rivers?

It is not widely known that St Francis wrote a Rule for Hermitages. He provided for a specific form of the eremitical life in the Franciscan Order in which three and not more than four friars may live together as hermits. The Rule begins with these words: 'Let those friars who want to lead the religious life in hermitages, do so in groups of three or at most four. Two of these are to be mothers and they are to have two sons or at least one. The two who are mothers are to lead the life of Martha; the two who are sons the life of Mary.' The best study of the Rule for Hermitages, which also gives a critical edition of the text, is K. Esser, OFM, 'Die Regula pro Eremitoriis data des Hl. Franziskus von Assisi' *Franziskanische Studien* 44 (1962) 383-417. T. Merton made some very interesting comments on this aspect of Franciscan life in *Contemplation in a World of Action* (London 1971), pp 260-268.

For an inspiring introduction to the Franciscan vision of the world A. Gemelli's exciting and comprehensive study remains a classic: *Il Francescanesimo* (Milan 1932). This book went into its second edition after only six months from its initial publication. The first part presents the life of St Francis and his spirituality. After this, one is led through the history of the Franciscan Order and its significance down to the nineteenth century. The third part treats of the relevance of Franciscan thought to the problems and questions of the early twentieth century.

Another excellent introduction to the significance and relevance of St Francis is the book by von Galli, SJ, *Gelebte Zukunft: Franz von Assisi* (Lucerne and Frankfurt/M 1970). Von Galli is concerned above all with the poverty of St Francis. St Francis stands before the world as a model of gospel poverty and he is an incentive to us to share what we have received so generously. In his love of poverty St Francis shows us a pathway to the future. On the meaning of the Franciscan way of life in the world of our time, L. Iriarte de Aspurz, OFMCap., presents a fine theological study: *Vocación Franciscana* (Madrid 1971). He examines the fundamental principles of the Franciscan charism and shows both their relevance and attractiveness. The heart of this book lies in the chapter on fraternity in which the author insists that it is essential to understand that St Francis first discovered his brother, that is, Jesus Christ, before he founded a brotherhood. In fact, in his discovery of Christ the Brother, St Francis realised that all creatures are a brotherhood.

An original and very instructive study of St Francis and his spirituality is the book by

A. van Corstanje, OFM, *Franciscus Bijbel der Armen* (Haarlem 1976). Reading this book convinces one that St Francis belongs to all humanity, he is a man for all seasons. His life was a living gospel, a visible gospel, as L. A. M. Goosens, OFM, says in his introduction. Van Corstanje leads us into the secret and mystery of St Francis, and his book bears witness that the evangelical virtues of voluntary poverty, obedience and humility are strong and courageous virtues and are the basis of hope for the future.

No bibliography that would seek to introduce St Francis can possibly omit the novel by N. Kazantzakis, *God's Pauper. St Francis of Assisi* (Oxford 1962). This is a translation from the original Greek, and it is found in a number of other translations. The book is not a historical biography; as the title says, it is a novel. As a novel it is a profound, inspiring and authentic interpretation of St Francis. Let then Kazantzakis have the last word in this essay. I quote from the final paragraph of his prologue:

for me Saint Francis is the model of the dutiful man, the man who by means of ceaseless, supremely cruel struggle succeeds in fulfilling our highest obligation, something higher even than morality or truth or beauty: the obligation to transubstantiate the matter which God entrusted to us, and turn it into spirit.

G

CONCLUSION

Christian Duquoc

à propos Francis,
the Theological Value of the Legend

FRANCIS OF ASSISI is not forgotten; the articles printed in this issue testify to the persistence of his influence. Francis is a man of the thirteenth century, and yet the gap in time, the cultural difference do not make him a stranger to us; he touches us, and many of our contemporaries may well have been converted to the gospel by him. Francis took up the challenges of his epoch with courage, serenity and an indestructible hope. We recognise in some of them the same questions that assail us. Not that we expect answers from him; it is rather that we have the presentiment that he opens up a quite new path for us.

Francis was not a theologian, any more than he was a man for doctrine or rule; he was a disciple of Jesus. This was how he was seen and how he passed into history. Not everything that is told about him belongs to scientific history. Scientific history is of its nature critical, it does not empower a person to pass beyond the density of history. Science does not create heroes or saints. This is precisely what legend does make possible. The legend of Francis has left an indelible imprint on the history of the West. It makes present again the action of Francis that as such is lost for ever; no exact and scientific report of Francis' deeds and gestures would have produced such a socio-historic effect. Without the legend, Francis would have been a Christian amongst others, he would not have been one of those people that have the power to make us get up and follow them. This gap between legend and scientific history, a gap that can be plotted at the level of socio-historic and religious effect, invites us to underline the necessity of the sort of theology that some people nowadays like to call 'narrative'.

Heroes exist only through legend: are the destinies of Guevara and Camillo Torres in Latin America imaginable without the exalted rumours that wrapped their personalities around and made their actions the symbols of the coming liberation? It is only the effect engraved in the collective memory that makes the hero. Not that I therefore mean to deny the reality of the courage they needed to take the risks they did. But it is less their courage that makes history than the story that noises it abroad. Some unknown soldier killed Goliath. Legend attributed this anti-Philistine act to David: it is the story that made David the hero. Scientific history can do its best to restore the act of courage to the unknown soldier, it cannot deprive David of his nimbus; he will linger in the memory as the conqueror of the Philistine, a title that opens up his dynasty to the grandiose destiny of which the prophets will speak.

There are authentic Christians who have changed the course of their time and yet remain unknown. Scholarly works can draw them out of their undeserved obscurity. Science becomes the last judgment. Research brings them out into the collective memory only in order to declare the vanity of its efforts: they return to the darkness whence they came. Without legend history is amusement, it brings back to life important or modest people, it does not create heroes or saints. It does not produce a collective memory. *Vox populi, vox Dei*, it used to be said. The Vatican does not create a saint, it acknowledges the force of the legend that attaches to a person.

Francis inhabits a legend, and that is why he inhabits our history. Fascinating stories have given universal value to an original attitude and a possibly subversive practice in the thirteenth century. Jesus came to have stories told about him, so did Francis. Both were as a result of this elaboration of stories given a considerable power in the social game. It is the power these conferred which is the inner explanation of the reflections that follow: reflections about eternism and classical theology, about the narrative difference, and about the story and transforming practice.

1. ETERNISM AND CLASSICAL THEOLOGY

Statues, icons, paintings declare holiness. They escape time or arrest it. To be a saint is to have the right to enter into the serenity of Romanesque or Gothic sculptures and into the hieratic order of Byzantine icons. The saint flees time. This sacred art reflects a glory that dwells outside our world, it radiates a light that issues from elsewhere.

Classical theology is the writing of this form of art: product of the ontological effort of the middle ages it is dedicated to the eternal and dwells there. It eliminates time, it is uninterested in the incidental. It poses questions about the essence of dogmas, virtues, Christianity. It is poverty, freedom, truth that nourishes its thinking, not the poor man, the free man, the truthful man. It makes models and paradigms pass in procession before our eyes as do the sculptures of our Romanesque churches or cathedrals; it fastens on examples, it outlines types. It keeps everything that happens or irrupts or is transformed outside its field of thought. Or, if it does give such things a glance, it is to freeze them.

Where are we to situate Francis in such a way of thinking? There would be room for him only if he were reduced to the status of an icon, a representation, an example, an illustration. Francis manifests Lady Poverty: he enables us to see the essence of poverty. The essence arrests the movement of the poor man, it passes over the act of revolt of the first self-stripping in the commercial city of Assisi. Essential poverty calls for contemplation, it does not invite action.

Thus the essence and the dream of classical theology, such as we have described it schematically and to some extent unfairly in this way, can express its eternal character in sculpted Gothic stone or in icons and yet it has a social basis and colludes with an ideology which the eternal serves to reinforce and consolidate. By remaining permanently in the 'same', eternity legitimates and strengthens social permanence. Nothing that is not a reflection of the eternal becomes worthy of thought and nothing that was not already eternal in its manifestations is worth traversing humankind's fleeting time. In this perspective Francis is identified with poverty, or, sometimes, with ecological innocence. He enthuses, fascinates, reassures us. He has risen into the heaven of Platonic ideals. We can contemplate his image: a reflection of the eternal beauty of the innocent beholding of beautiful nature and the simple gospel. The image confirms everybody in his place: everything is adjusted. The essence of poverty is real, we can honour it as we honour the love of Christ. Even the wolf of Gubbio can discern the eternal.

There is a complicity between the arrest of time, its exorcism in medieval painting or sculpture, and the fashioning of concepts representing the eternal: everything is in its place as long as time moves only incidentally. Everything is serene if the models of virtue are open to heaven and are thus manifested in examples to hand, if the real assures the victory of this fallen world against time.

To define the essence of the virtue of poverty or that of the gospel and to explore their concept is to fail Francis. He was not an icon, a picturesque personage, an epiphany of the eternal, an instance or a model. As long as he is part of an order in which time and history are a disturbing other to be got rid of, Francis is effectively rejected, even if he is honoured. Canonisation can amount to rendering him banal. In short, he has no place in classical theology, he inhabits legend and not the world of representation.

2. THE NARRATIVE DIFFERENCE

Francis inhabits legend. Let us recall Francis de Beer's article about the meeting of Francis and the Sultan. This meeting astonished his contemporaries. They attempted to exorcise it by transcribing it into their frame of reference. In point of fact this meeting fitted into no frame of reference because it did not share the interests of the crusades. This crusade was, for both Christian and Muslim, part of the cosmic struggle of Good and Evil, the precise location of which each partner was convinced he knew. Everything was in place because the soldier who wielded the sword was armed by the arm of the God.

Francis meets the Sultan to shatter the apocalyptic clarity of the combat, he denies the geography of Good and Evil, God arms neither the Muslim nor the Christian soldier. They arm themselves for interests that are not those of God. In this way time intrudes, the eternism of order is rejected. By his gesture, Francis makes a history possible.

A comparison between this gesture of Francis with what report attributes to Dominic in his fight against the Cathars, the recourse to the Inquisition—which was finally to mark the policy of intolerance towards those who rejected official thinking— is a measure of the gap between the gesture of Francis that had no echo in the logic of its epoch and the act of Dominic that had only too many resonances in the dominant social relationship of his time. Francis opens out into the hope of breaking the inexorable repetition of the struggle between Good and Evil, an abstract struggle if ever there was one, whereas Dominic remains within the opposition between Truth and Error that generates intolerance and destruction. We remember the gesture of Francis, we do our best to forget the epic of the Crusade against the Cathars: it is only one instance of a battle repeated a hundred times over and in such a way that the partners are representatives, types.

The story breaks with the eternism of classical theology: it records acts inscribed in time that make something other than eternal figures ensuring the survival of an immutable order appear in history. Francis does not illustrate the adventures of Lady Poverty: he chooses to be poor in the particular context of a new class of rising commercial bourgeois, at a moment when the bonds of feudal society are losing their grip. It is not poverty as such that is important, it is the action that transforms the relationship imposed by the powerful and the rich, that reveals the latent idolatry of their behaviour. What Francis does and what the story takes up time and again is unrepeatable, what he does is unique. One does not strip twice in front of a bishop or one's father: the act would become theatrical. It therefore seems to me to be illusory for an order or an institution to manifest the permanence of poverty by the observance of a rule. Poverty has no essence that can be embodied in a rule: it either falls short of the situation, or else it becomes the theatrical, relapses into the order of representation, it ceases to be creative, action. It is possible to recall acts that were subversive, it is impossible to institutionalise them as norms. Such acts open out into creativity if they are told as stories. Turned into laws, they lose their relevance. The story form is the guarantee of their real power.

The consequences for an order which monopolises the inheritance in an institution seem to me to be formidable. How can one make a profession and a vocation of poverty? Does this amount to making a legalisable essence out of it, to condemning oneself to deduce an action from an essence? Fortunately, legend or story has made it possible to put a creative distance between the primordial gesture and the inheritance. If Francis were only the rule, he would have no relevance for us. He would suffer the fate of so many founders of congregations that wear themselves out by seeking to reactualise their origin. Without a legend one kills oneself interpreting and adapting constitutions. In this aspect institutional law joins classical theology: it eternalises. This is why we have the spectacle, especially since Vatican II, of orders and congregations which have no legend running after time. One chapter after another, one constitution after another serve only to measure irrelevance: norms do not make a gesture. Orders and congregations die: freezing the experience of an instant in the deceptive eternism of a law, they lose the capacity to live time, to make history: they have exorcised it from the start.

The history of the Franciscan heritage with its quarrels, its mutual outbiddings, its splits, its renewals, testifies to the necessity of a legend. It is the telling of the story of the gesture of Francis which gives the heritage the power to traverse time and to be creative. It is not constitutions, not norms that do this. A movement without a legend spends its energy in ensuring its survival.

These few reflections show that there is the suggestion of a complicity between an institutional law that escapes from time and a theology that finds truth in some atemporal essence. An institutional law and a classical theology that aim to attain the divine in stability and that set legend and story aside as of minor importance acts as supporters of those who profit by history. The poor and the rejected of this world have no hope here. The story of the action of Jesus, like that of the gestures of Francis, does not allow the eternal to tame revolt.

3. STORY AND TRANSFORMING PRACTICE

The legend of Francis cannot be integrated into a right of inheritance or an essentialist philosophy of poverty. I reiterate: the action of Francis stripping himself in front of his bishop and his father is unrepeatable except in a theatrical manner. Such an act is of its nature unforeseeable, unexplainable. The form of the story maintains this distance: Francis made this gesture once and for all. The story therefore opens up other possibilities: the logic of the new world of commerce did not call forth this gesture. The story records the unforeseeable. And in doing so, it promotes the unforeseeable in other times and in other places.

Everything could have seemed in order to Francis. His family, cultural and religious circumstances traced out an honourable path. He could have lived it in a Christian manner by being his father's honest successor. He could, without denying his Christianity, have made his own the disputes with the other cities: many knights of the time did just that and nobody thought of saying that they were not Christians. He could just as honourably have departed for the Crusade, drawn his sword in that cause, achieved many feats of prowess: nobody would have dreamt of seeing a defiance of Christian ideals in all this. On the contrary, he would have returned covered with glory, he would have been lauded for having been so courageous as to deliver the tomb of Christ from the hands of the infidel.

Francis introduced the unforeseeable, and the unforeseeable consisted in the revolt against the logic of a class, a city, a civilisation. Francis was Christian, but he was Christian in quite a different way from that of his contemporaries. The gesture of Francis stripping himself breaks the certainties held by the majority, the habits of centuries, received convictions. Time reasserts its rights—and doing so, with Francis it makes men perceive the creative power inherent in their liberty, and even more so in the spirit issued from the gospel.

The legend of Francis is like the passion of Jesus. Many people have an interest in trivialising it, in making it part of the logical order of expiation, of the debt to be paid, in transforming it into a response to the necessity of a balance between sin and grace. The exploiters and the profiteers are reassured: all can complain equally about their sinful destiny, everybody carries the penalty of his sins. The passion as a theory accredits the permanence of sin as well as the permanence of pardon. The innocent man who died has washed everything, so everything can carry on as before. Everything stays the same: the profiteers can continue to squeeze their profits, the exploiters to extract their gains. The passion has been transformed into the paradigm of the eternal game of life and death, good and evil, mercy and justice. The passion retells the complaint against our natural destiny. The transformation consists in slipping from story to explanation: the talk is of death, not of the death of Jesus as a result of a legal proceedings; the talk is of sin, not of the sin of the leaders of the people. Now everybody can read the text translated in this way: it generates nothing, it does not produce a new history.

The day the rejected, the exploited read the text, however, they give it back its story form, they wrest it from the theory or from the translation which hides it. For then the personages that appear are not eternal figures locked in a cosmic combat. It is the champion of the freedom of the rejected who is rejected; it is a fighter for the non-exclusion of the excluded who is excluded; it is an opponent of violence who is violated. Not by eternal figures, but by such and such men, placed in such and such a position and having such and such interests. The story takes on a transforming power. It supports revolt against resignation. It unlocks the power of history to us, it exorcises natural fatalism. The story assumes a subversive potential when it is wrestled from essentialist explanation. The story encourages action, it carries an invitation to prolong its own movement.

The legend of Francis is no exception to this double movement: either the repetition of an explanation which renders it impotent or the continuation of a story which makes it subversive. The inheritance operates at these two opposed levels: either the poverty of Francis is a manifestation, it fascinates and it freezes; or else it is an action, it invites us to make history ourselves. It is the reader of the legend who decides between one interpretation and another—but only the person who reads it as an invitation to prolong the legend respects the text. The other sort of reader, for his own reasons, strives to empty it of its power. The eternism of the explanation to which he refers has as its social aim to deprive the gospel of its transfiguring power: it neutralises interests implicit in the movement of the legend.

Francis is not an object of theology, he is the hero of a legend, a saint of the Church. Theologies that reduce the legend to the function of illustrating eternal virtues banish the power that comes from the Franciscan gesture, they legitimate a heritage in drawing its subversive sting, they postulate a rite, they make Francis the subject-matter of a cult. Institutional law colludes with them. But legend resists: recalling to mind the unforeseeable action it incites people to creative renewal by its narrative openness. Perhaps the really timely thing would be to sacrifice less at the altar of the theory of narrativity and to create and recite legends.

Translated by John Maxwell

Contributors

FRANCIS DE BEER, O.F.M., was born in 1921 in Roubaix, Belgium, and is a Franciscan. From 1948 to 1957 he was professor of philosophy at the Franciscan scholasticate at Lille and director of lectures on spirituality at the Catholic Faculties of Lille. He holds a diploma in higher studies in philosophy and a doctorate in religious studies from the University of Strasbourg. He is currently attached to the Strasbourg Centre for Franciscan Studies and is a spiritual counsellor for religious congregations. His most recent publications are *Prière et Philosophie, La Première Rencontre de Claire et François d'Assise* (1979), *Les Augustines au Pays-Bas Français depuis le X° Siècle* (1981).

THÉOPHILE DESBONNETS, O.F.M., entered the Franciscan Order in 1943 and was ordained priest in 1950. Since 1965 he has specialised more particularly in the medieval Franciscan sources and his publications on the subject include a critical edition of the *Legenda trium sociorum*.

ERIC DOYLE, O.F.M., was born in Bolton, England, in 1938. He entered the Franciscan Order in 1954 and was ordained priest in 1961. He studied in Rome where he received the doctorate in theology in 1964. Since that time he has taught in the Franciscan House of Studies in the English Province of the Order of Friars Minor. He is a member of the department of graduate theology at St Bonaventure University, New York, where he teaches in the summer.

He was a member of the Anglican/Roman Catholic Working Group on the ordination of women which met in Assisi in November 1975 and of the Anglican/Roman Catholic Consultation on the ordination of women which met at Versailles in February 1978.

He broadcasts frequently on BBC Radio and on Independent Television. He has given retreats to priests and religious all over Great Britain.

He has published scholarly articles on theological, spiritual and historic subjects in *Speculum*, *Archivum Franciscanum Historicum*, *Franciscan Studies*, *The Clergy Review*, *Review for Religious*, *The Tablet*, *The Sower*, *Doctrine and Life* and *Religious Life Reviews*. His book *St Francis and the Song of Brotherhood*, which is an approach to the ecological crisis through the teaching on fraternity contained in *The Canticle of Brother Sun*, was a best-seller in England. It has just been published in an American edition. At the moment he is finishing an edition of St Bonaventure's sermons on St Francis in English and is preparing a book on Christology based on the central idea of meaning.

BERTRAND DUCLOS, O.F.M., was born in 1917 in the Pyrenees. He entered the Franciscan province of Toulouse in 1945; there his duties have included instruction, work at the students' chaplaincy of Toulouse, editing the journal *Frères du Monde* and being provincial minister. He is now at Béziers, the chaplain of a lycée and leader of a centre for continuing formation.

CHRISTIAN DUQUOC, O.P., was born in 1926 in Nantes, France. He was ordained to the priesthood in 1953. He did his studies at the Dominican *studium* of Leysse, France, the University of Fribourg, Switzerland, the faculties of Le Saulchoir, France, and the Ecole Biblique, Jerusalem. Graduate of the Ecole Biblique and doctor in theology as he is, he now teaches dogma in the theological faculty in Lyons and is a member of the editorial committee of *Lumière et Vie*. His publications include *L'Eglise et le progrès* and *Christologie* (2 vols. 1972).

NAZARENO FABBRETTI, O.F.M., was born at Pistoia on 1 January 1920. Ordained priest in 1943, he has taught contemporary literature in the Institutes of the Order. He contributes to religious and lay daily papers and periodicals (*Jesus, L'Europeo, La Domenica del Corriere*, etc.). Among his books are *Nessuno* (1953), *I servi inutili* (in collaboration) (1954), *Don Mazzolari, Don Milani, i 'disobbedienti'* (1969), *Francesco* (1977), *Francesco e altro* (ed.) (1977). With Luigi Santucci he edited *Francesco otto secoli* (Mondadori) for the eighth centenary of the birth of Francis of Assisi.

JACQUES LE GOFF was born in 1924 and studied at the Ecole Normale Supérieur. He then studied history at the French School in Rome, was appointed to Lille University, and has been director of studies in the Ecole des Hautes Etudes en Sciences Sociales since 1962, following Lucien Febvre and Fernand Braudel as president of the school from 1972-7. His books include *Marchands et Banquiers du Moyen Age* (1956), *Les Intellectuels au Moyen Age* (1957), *Pour un autre Moyen Age* (1977) and *La Naissance du Purgatoire* (1981).

MICHEL MOLLAT was born at Ancenis (Loire Atlantique). He has a teaching degree (*agrégé*) in history and geography and a doctorate in literature; he now teaches at the Sorbonne and is a member of the Institut de France. His most recent publications are: *Genèse médiévale de la France moderne* (XIVe-XVe siecles) (Grenoble 1970; paperback edn. Paris 1977); *Ongles Bleus, Jacques et Ciompi. Les révolutions populaires en Europe aux XIVe et XVe siècles* (with Philippe Wolff) (Paris 1970; English edn. London 1973); *Etudes sur l'économie et la société de l'Occident médiéval* (XIIe-XVes) (collection of articles published in various French and foreign journals) (London 1977); *Etudes sur l'histoire de la Pauvreté (Moyen Age—XVIes)* (seminary studies edited by the author) 2 vols (Paris 1977); *Les pauvres au Moyen Age—Etude social* (Paris 1978; English edn. forthcoming).

ANTON ROTZETTER, O.F.M., is a Capuchin. Born in 1939 in Basle, Switzerland, he was ordained priest in 1964. He studied at his Order's Institute at Solothurn and at the theological faculties of Fribourg, Bonn and Tübingen, gaining a licentiate and doctorate in theology. He is a lecturer in Franciscan theology and spirituality and director of the Institute for Spirituality at the Franciscan and Capuchin Institute for Philosophical and Theological Studies at Münster. He is active in adult religious education and in giving retreats. His publications include: *Die Funktion der franziskanischen Bewegung in der Kirche. Eine pastoraltheologische Interpretation der grundlegenden franziskanischen Texte* (1977); with E. Hug *Franz von Assisi, Die Demut Gottes. Meditationen, Lieder, Gebete* (1977, 1978, 1980); with H. Krämer *Bist Du es, der en Steinen die Härte nimmt. Legenden* (1978); with H. Krämer *Den Gedanken eine Treppe, den Füssen ein Weg* (1979); with E. Hug *Aegidius von Assisi, Die Weisheit des Einfachen* (1980); editor *Geist wird Leib. Theologische und anthropologische Voraussetzungen des geistlichen Lebens. Seminar Spiritualität 1* (1979); editor *Geist und Geistesgaben. Die Erscheinungsformen des geistlichen Lebens in ihrer Einheit und Vielfalt* (1980).

KNUT WALF was born in Berlin in 1936 and was ordained in 1962. He studied philosophy, theology, jurisprudence and canon law in Fribourg (Switzerland) and Munich, where he qualified as a doctor and as a university lecturer. From 1966 until 1968, he was active in pastoral work in West Berlin. In 1972 he became a university teacher, teaching canon law at Munich, where he became director of the Institute of Canon Law in 1974. In 1977, he was appointed to the chair of canon law at the University of Nijmegen. In addition to articles in journals and contributions to symposia he has written *Die Entwicklung des päpstlichen Gesandtschaftswesens in dem Zeitabschnitt zwischen Dekretalrecht und Wiener Kongress* (1159-1815) (1966); *Das bischöfliche Amt in der Sicht josephischer Kirchenrechtler* (1975); co-author M. Pilters, *Menschenrechte in der Kirche* (1980).

CONCILIUM

Claude Geffré. 0 8164 2542 6 144pp.

87. **The Future of Christian Marriage.** Ed. William Bassett and Peter Huizing. 0 8164 2575 2.

88. **Polarization in the Church.** Ed. Hans Küng and Walter Kasper. 0 8164 2572 8 156pp.

89. **Spiritual Revivals.** Ed. Christian Duquoc and Casiano Floristán. 0 8164 2573 6 156pp.

90. **Power and the Word of God.** Ed. Franz Bockle and Jacques Marie Pohier. 0 8164 2574 4 156pp.

91. **The Church as Institution.** Ed. Gregory Baum and Andrew Greeley. 0 8164 2575 2 168pp.

92. **Politics and Liturgy.** Ed. Herman Schmidt and David Power. 0 8164 2576 0 156pp.

93. **Jesus Christ and Human Freedom.** Ed. Edward Schillebeeckx and Bas van Iersel. 0 8164 2577 9 168pp.

94. **The Experience of Dying.** Ed. Norbert Greinacher and Alois Müller. 0 8164 2578 7 156pp.

95. **Theology of Joy.** Ed. Johannes Baptist Metz and Jean-Pierre Jossua. 0 8164 2579 5 164pp.

96. **The Mystical and Political Dimension of the Christian Faith.** Ed. Claude Geffré and Gustavo Guttierez. 0 8164 2580 9 168pp.

97. **The Future of the Religious Life.** Ed. Peter Huizing and William Bassett. 0 8164 2094 7 96pp.

98. **Christians and Jews.** Ed. Hans Küng and Walter Kasper. 0 8164 2095 5 96pp.

99. **Experience of the Spirit.** Ed. Peter Huizing and William Bassett. 0 8164 2096 3 144pp.

100. **Sexuality in Contemporary Catholicism.** Ed. Franz Bockle and Jacques Marie Pohier. 0 8164 2097 1 126pp.

101. **Ethnicity.** Ed. Andrew Greeley and Gregory Baum. 0 8164 2145 5 120pp.

102. **Liturgy and Cultural Religious Traditions.** Ed. Herman Schmidt and David Power. 0 8164 2146 2 120pp.

103. **A Personal God?** Ed. Edward Schillebeeckx and Bas van Iersel. 0 8164 2149 8 142pp.

104. **The Poor and the Church.** Ed. Norbert Greinacher and Alois Müller. 0 8164 2147 1 128pp.

105. **Christianity and Socialism.** Ed. Johannes Baptist Metz and Jean-Pierre Jossua. 0 8164 2148 X 144pp.

106. **The Churches of Africa: Future Prospects.** Ed. Claude Geffré and Bertrand Luneau. 0 8164 2150 1 128pp.

107. **Judgement in the Church.** Ed. William Bassett and Peter Huizing. 0 8164 2166 8 128pp.

108. **Why Did God Make Me?** Ed. Hans Küng and Jürgen Moltmann. 0 8164 2167 6 112pp.

109. **Charisms in the Church.** Ed. Christian Duquoc and Casiano Floristán. 0 8164 2168 4 128pp.

110. **Moral Formation and Christianity.** Ed. Franz Bockle and Jacques Marie Pohier. 0 8164 2169 2 120pp.

111. **Communication in the Church.** Ed. Gregory Baum and Andrew Greeley. 0 8164 2170 6 126pp.

112. **Liturgy and Human Passage.** Ed. David Power and Luis Maldonado. 0 8164 2608 2 136pp.

113. **Revelation and Experience.** Ed. Edward Schillebeeckx and Bas van Iersel. 0 8164 2609 0 134pp.

114. **Evangelization in the World Today.** Ed. Norbert Greinacher and Alois Müller. 0 8164 2610 4 136pp.

115. **Doing Theology in New Places.** Ed. Jean-Pierre Jossua and Johannes Baptist Metz. 0 8164 2611 2 120pp.

116. **Buddhism and Christianity.** Ed. Claude Geffré and Mariasusai Dhavamony. 0 8164 2612 0 136pp.

117. **The Finances of the Church.** Ed. William Bassett and Peter Huizing. 0 8164 2197 8 160pp.

118. **An Ecumenical Confession of Faith?** Ed. Hans Küng and Jürgen Moltmann. 0 8164 2198 6 136pp.

119. **Discernment of the Spirit and of Spirits.** Ed. Casiano Floristán and Christian Duquoc. 0 8164 2199 4 136pp.

120. **The Death Penalty and Torture.** Ed. Franz Bockle and Jacques Marie Pohier. 0 8164 2200 1 136pp.

121. **The Family in Crisis or in Transition.** Ed. Andrew Greely. 0 567 30001 3 128pp.

122. **Structures of Initiation in Crisis.** Ed. Luis Maldonado and David Power. 0 567 30002 1 128pp.

123. **Heaven.** Ed. Bas van Iersel and Edward Schillebeeckx. 0 567 30003 X 120pp.

124. **The Church and the Rights of Man.** Ed. Alois Müller and Norbert Greinacher. 0 567 30004 8 140pp.

125. **Christianity and the Bourgeoisie.** Ed. Johannes Baptist Metz. 0 567 30005 6 142pp.

126. **China as a Challenge to the Church.** Ed. Claude Geffré and Joseph Spae. 0 567 30006 4 136pp.

127. **The Roman Curia and the Communion of Churches.** Ed. Peter Huizing and Knut Walf. 0 567 30007 2 144pp.

128. **Conflicts about the Holy Spirit.** Ed. Hans Küng and Jürgen Moltmann. 0 567 30008 0 144pp.

129. **Models of Holiness.** Ed. Christian Duquoc and Casiano Floristán. 0 567 30009 9 128pp.

130. **The Dignity of the Despised of the Earth.** Ed. Jacques Marie Pohier and Dietmar Mieth. 0 567 30010 2 144pp.

131. **Work and Religion.** Ed. Gregory Baum. 0 567 30011 0 148pp.

132. **Symbol and Art in Worship.** Ed. Luis Maldonado and David Power. 0 567 30012 9 136pp.

133. **Right of the Community to a Priest.** Ed. Edward Schillebeeckx and Johannes Baptist Metz. 0 567 30013 7 148pp.

134. **Women in a Men's Church.** Ed. Virgil Elizondo and Norbert Greinacher. 0 567 30014 5 144pp.

135. **True and False Universality of Christianity.** Ed. Claude Geffré and Jean-Pierre Jossua. 0 567 30015 3 138pp.

136. **What is Religion? An Inquiry for Christian Theology.** Ed. Mircea Eliade and David Tracy. 0 567 30016 1 98pp.

137. **Electing our Own Bishops.** Ed. Peter Huizing and Knut Walf. 0 567 30017 X 112pp.

138. **Conflicting Ways of Interpreting the Bible.** Ed. Hans Küng and Jürgen Moltmann. 0 567 30018 8 112pp.

139. **Christian Obedience.** Ed. Casiano Floristán and Christian Duquoc. 0 567 30019 6 96pp.

140. **Christian Ethics and Economics: the North-South Conflict.** Ed. Dietmar Mieth and Jacques Marie Pohier. 0 567 30020 X 128pp.

1981

141. **Neo-Conservatism: Social and Religious Phenomenon.** Ed. Gregory Baum and John Coleman. 0 567 30021 8.

142. **The Times of Celebration.** Ed. David Power and Mary Collins. 0 567 30022 6.

143. **God and Father.** Ed. Edward Schillebeeckx and Johannes Baptist Metz. 0 567 30023 4.

144. **Tensions Between the Churches of the First World and the Third World.** Ed. Virgil Elizondo and Norbert Greinacher. 0 567 30024 2.

145. **Nietzsche and Christianity.** Ed. Claude Geffré and Jean-Pierre Jossua. 0 567 30025 0.

146. **Where Does the Church Stand?** Ed. Giuseppe Alberigo. 0 567 30026 9.

147. **The Revised Code of Canon Law: a Missed Opportunity?** Ed. Peter Huizing and Knut Walf. 0 567 30027 7.

148. **Who Has the Say in the Church?** Ed. Hans Küng and Jürgen Moltmann. 0 567 30028 5.

149. **Francis of Assisi: an Example?** Ed. Casiano Floristán and Christian Duquoc. 0 567 30029 3.

150. **One Faith, One Church, Many Moralities?** Ed. Jacques Pohier and Dietmar Mieth. 0 567 30030 7.

All back issues are still in print and available for sale. Orders should be sent to the publishers,

T. & T. CLARK LIMITED

36 George Street, Edinburgh EH2 2LQ, Scotland